RO
CROI

D1586868

AN ILLUSTRATED
ARCHITECTURAL
GUIDE

FOREWARDS, like Editorials, give the reader a kick-start into
the body of a book. However, unlike the dictionary definition
which would indicate that a foreward is indeed in advance of
anything else written, it perhaps should be thought of as a
'backward', the cart of hindsight placed before the horse of
vision. Luckily, hindsight can rest easily here as this guide keeps
the same high standards as the others in its series and since
Ross & Cromarty is one of the most diverse of all Scottish
counties, its architecture reflects this in a northern wealth of
buildings which are succinctly displayed both in text and
photographs. This is a book that should be kept in the car and
read like a map; each turn of the road reveals something new
and the Guide will enliven even a familiar journey by putting
structure to what is now a ruin and detail to the kaleidoscopic
styles that span this part of Scotland.

Cromartie

THE EARL OF CROMARTIE

©Author: Elizabeth Beaton
Series editor: Charles McKean
Series consultant: David Walker
Cover design: Dorothy Steedman
Editorial consultant: Duncan McAra

Royal Incorporation of Architects in Scotland
ISBN 1873190 04 2
First Published 1992

Cover illustrations:
Mellon Charles (photo C McKean)
The Retreat, Cromarty (photo E Beaton)

Typesetting, page make-up and picture scans:
Almond Design, Edinburgh
Printed by Pillans & Wilson Ltd, Edinburgh

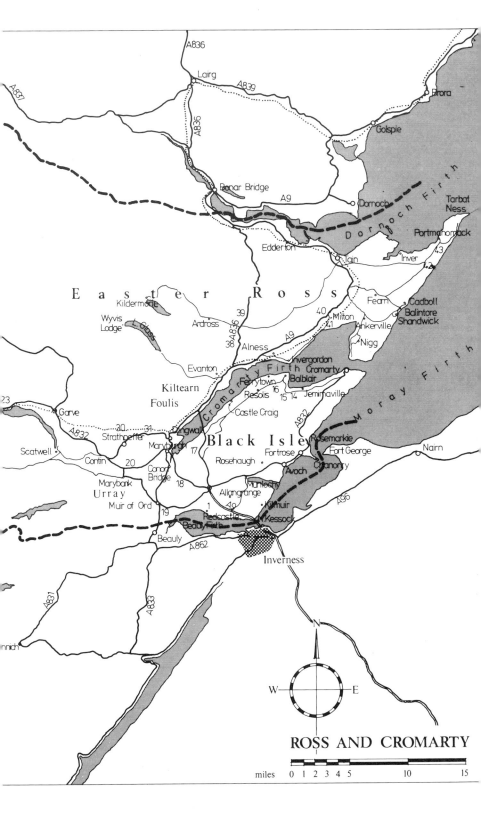

ROSS AND CROMARTY

Ross and Cromarty spans northern Scotland east to west. On the east, the low-lying Tarbat peninsula of Easter Ross and the steep cliffs of the Sutors guard the narrow entrance to the Cromarty Firth; to the west the lands of Coigach, Gairloch and Applecross are separated by wide bays and deep lochs with a scatter of small islands. The scenery is ever varied and always beautiful, made up of hills and valleys, moors and rivers, farmland and woods, lochs and sea. In the east the rich farmlands of the Black Isle and Easter Ross slope gently to the Beauly, Cromarty and Dornoch Firths, the fields interspersed with woodland. Sheltered valleys with fast-flowing rivers cut deep into the hinterland, the glens slicing into the uplands. The bare hills and moors of the central massif, splattered with lochs and burns, dip westwards to a dramatic coastline, serrated by deep sea lochs and fringed by narrow belts of arable land and scattered crofting townships. Tracks through valley and over hill indicate former passes once important lines of communication and now used only by stalkers and walkers. Innumerable ferry sites, on both east and west coasts, recall the importance of these inland waters as bridges rather than barriers.

Roads were constructed through glens from early 19th century; the Commission for Highland Roads and Bridges, established in 1803, was largely responsible for much of the network we use today and many fine bridges spanning fast rivers, previously crossed at considerable risk if at all. Over the past three decades impressive viaducts and bridges have been built to carry the A9 over the **Kessock**

RCAHMS

Thatched cottage, Lonbain, Applecross

Opposite *The Paye, Cromarty (photo Elizabeth Beaton)*

Below *Strathpeffer.*
Bottom *Contin Bridge, 1812-13*

Historic Scotland

Beaton

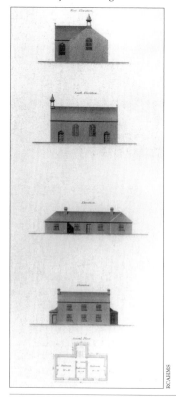

Highland churches and manses:
Thomas Telford drawings

RCAHMS

Narrows linking Inverness with Ross and Cromarty and to span both the **Cromarty** and **Dornoch Firths**.

The railway network came into being in the 1860s and 1870s, north from Inverness via Dingwall to Wick and Thurso and westwards from Dingwall to Kyle of Lochalsh. In 1872 Cromarty was linked to Muir of Ord by 22 miles of railway and a decade later the branch line between Dingwall and Strathpeffer connected the spa with the main line from the south to encourage tourist traffic. Both these lines are now closed, leaving visitors to wonder at the occasional 'Station Hotel' or 'Station Road' where there is no evidence of a railway.

The double-barrelled name of the District, Ross and Cromarty, is derived from the amalgamated counties of Ross-shire and Cromartyshire. The latter was very fragmented, stemming from landownership of the Urquharts of Cromarty and subsequently the Mackenzie Earls of Cromartie (note different spelling), and was absorbed into Ross-shire by the end of the 19th century. The current District is slightly smaller than the former county, lacking parishes bordering Loch Duich in the west, Kincardine in Strathcarron on the Sutherland border and Lewis in the Outer Hebrides. The name Ross-shire and the geographical divisions of Easter and Wester Ross and the Black Isle remain in everyday use.

Cairns and **forts** record pre-Christian settlement. Irish St Maelrubha established a monastery at **Applecross** in 673 and **Fearn Abbey**, **Tain Collegiate Church** and **Fortrose Cathedral** became important medieval ecclesiastical foundations. Most parish churches date only from the 18th and 19th centuries but, like Fearn Abbey, some retain medieval fabric and many are on medieval sites. These churches vary from simple rectangular boxes lit by plain windows to ornate Gothic Revival and Italianate.

Increased population in the sometimes vast Highland parishes, with sizeable crofting townships in distant glens or far-flung coastal fishing villages, led to the 1823 Act for Building Additional Places of Worship in the Highlands and Islands of Scotland providing

£50,000 with which to provide church and manse at forty different sites. The Commission for Highland Roads and Bridges administered the project: its principal engineer Thomas Telford, with his assistants, produced designs for a church and two manses, one single, one two-storey, to cost £1500 together excluding land. These 'Parliamentary' churches and manses, to a standard pattern of church, with flexibility to accommodate larger congregations by the insertion of a gallery, became familiar architectural landmarks in the Highlands and Islands.

Above *Panelled door to 'Parliamentary' church, Poolewe.* Below *Mackenzie Place, former Avoch Episcopal School.* Bottom *Redcastle*

The discontent within the Church of Scotland in mid 19th century, exacerbated by rural over-population and land-hunger, is difficult to comprehend over a hundred years later in a more secular age. Sufficient that the vexed subject of patronage and choice of ministers came to a head in 1843 when the 'Disruption' tore the Church apart most particularly in the Highlands where the greater proportion of the ministers 'came out', abandoning manse, home and security. They worshipped with large supportive congregations in barns and caves or in the open air, those congregations building and financing new Free churches in an extraordinarily short time. The Free Church of Scotland became (as it remains) a strong force in the north. The unification of the Church of Scotland (the Auld Kirk) with the United Free Church in 1929 left many parishes with two buildings which they could ill afford to maintain.

The Education Act of 1872 led to the building of many new **schools** in both town and country. Later 20th-century changes in education, particularly the creation of modern secondary schools, have initiated a resurgence in school building.

Castles survive in many guises. The wooded mound of **Ormond** or **Ladyhill** overlooking the Moray Firth was once a medieval stronghold; there are roofless 15th- and 16th-century towers and castles at **Fairburn** and **Ballone**. Similar structures have been masked by the building accretions of many centuries, keeping their flavour but developing into castle-wise country mansions at **Balnagown**

Top Foulis Castle.
Above Church Street, Cromarty

One-and-a-half-storey house, Torridon

and **Kilcoy**. **Flowerdale House** (1738) stands on a former moated site while **Foulis Castle** is an 18th-century mansion which retains the title of its immediate predecessor. These castles were the seats of the dominant families, the Rosses, Mackenzies, Munros and Urquharts.

Imposing tolbooths in the principal towns of **Tain**, **Dingwall** and **Cromarty** are indicative of their historic civic and judicial importance, just as banks, shops and merchants' houses are the architectural witness of commercial activity.

The Black Isle and Easter Ross are richly endowed with smaller 18th-century houses, many built by those who made money in law and commerce. Immense farming improvements took place from the end of the 18th century as Easter Ross (together with the Lothians) was in the forefront of agricultural advances. Farm holdings were consolidated, land re-organised and new buildings constructed. Sturdy stone steadings with arcaded cart bays tell their own story of farm development, superseded by massive storage units and silage towers of the 20th century. Large ventilated barns peculiar to the west coast evolved to shelter hay and straw, thresh grain and provide storage in the wet climate. On the east coast there is an unusual concentration of **girnals** or **estate storehouses**, designed to receive and store the rent of grain and meal paid in kind by small farmers and crofters, subsequently exported by sea to urban markets to realise cash.

Traditional **one-and-a-half-storey houses** with gabled dormers abound. **Cottages** with slate or corrugated iron roofs are still common, if occasionally marred by unsuitable enlarged windows, but the small **thatched cottage** is now a rarity.

In this lovely, predominantly rural area, **industrial buildings** nonetheless play or have played their part in its prosperity: woollen mills, handsome bridges and viaducts, fishing stores, icehouses, harbours, lighthouses, railways, monumental Scottish Hydro-Electric generating stations.

This Guide identifies the architecture and buildings connected with this heritage. They reflect and record ecclesiastical changes and social patterns, the working life, domestic habits, poverty and wealth of people and patrons and constitute a social, cultural and economic history of Ross and Cromarty.

The Guide is divided into three sections – namely the Black Isle, Easter Ross and Wester Ross. Each of the three has a short introduction outlining the nature of the place. Towns, villages or location merit a brief introduction, followed by details of principal buildings. These are entered in order of name (or street number), date and architect (if known), followed by description. Neighbouring or associated buildings are included within these paragraphs. The small columns contain notes and quotations to expand and enliven the history and setting. There is an illustrated architectural glossary and an index at the end.

Toll House, Conon Bridge

The Guide begins on the south coast of the **Black Isle** at Redcastle, proceeding via Kilmuir and Avoch to Fortrose, Rosemarkie and Chanonry. From there to Cromarty, Resolis and along the northern coast skirting the Cromarty Firth to Ferintosh and Millbuie. The **Easter Ross** section starts at Muir of Ord, proceeding through Conon Bridge, Urray, Contin, Strath Conon, Kinlochluichart and Garve to Strathpeffer, whence it tracks the Peffery valley past Castle Leod and Fodderty to Dingwall. Foulis, Evanton and Alness follow with a digression via Struie and Strath Rusdale to Ardross and Kildermorie. Invergordon, Balnagown and Milton are succeeded by villages on the Fearn seaboard such as Nigg, Cadboll and Portmahomack, finishing with Tain, its environs and Edderton.

Wester Ross starts with Ullapool, then north and west to Isle Martin, Coigach and Tanera More. Inverlael and Strath More follow eastwards from Ullapool, the route hugging the coast south through Dundonnell to Gruinard and the Gairloch, small settlements including Aultbea and Poolewe, and important estates such as Inverewe and Flowerdale. The book ends with Kerrysdale and Loch Maree, Torridon, Applecross, Kishorn and Lochcarron.

Shandwick Stone, an ornate Pictish cross slab

Coigach, salmon cobles at Badentarbet

Maps
Principal locations are named on the front map; there are street maps of the principal towns. The reference numbers relate to the numbers in the text and not to page numbers.

Access
Many of the buildings described in this Guide are open to the public or visible from a public road or footpath. Some are private and, in remote areas, are approached by private roads. Readers are requested to respect the occupiers' privacy.

Acknowledgements
Many people and organisations have contributed to the preparation of this Guide and are listed on p.105. Publication to allow for a reasonably priced Guide has been made possible through the generous support of Ross & Cromarty District Council, Ross & Cromarty Heritage Society, Ross & Cromarty Enterprise, Highland Regional Council, the Northern Studies Centre, the Gairloch Museum and BP Exploration.

The maps have been prepared by Donald Canavan and Calum McKenzie by courtesy of the Law & Dunbar-Nasmith Partnership, Forres.

Black Isle

Bounded by the Moray Firth to the south and Cromarty Firth to the north, the fertile Black Isle is a peninsula rather than an island, farmland interspersed with deciduous and coniferous woods. The name 'Black Isle' is a misnomer; in spring and summer the predominant colour is that of green fields and woodland set against a blue sea, the green turning to gold later in the year as the grain ripens and the trees acquire their rich autumnal colouring. Some will say that the name originated in winter when the long 'whale-back' profile of the land mass stands out dark against a snowy backdrop of Ross-shire and Sutherland hills, others that the name comes from a corrupted Gaelic form of St Duthac's isle.

The Moray and Cromarty Firths have long provided the safest marine havens in the north-east, numerous ferries forming a sea link with Inverness-shire, Nairnshire and Moray to the south and Sutherland to the north. Rather than barriers, the firths have been marine bridges, attracting settlement from pre-Christian times until the present. The siting of most parish churches and burial grounds close to the shore recalls how people came by boat both to worship and to bury their dead. The sea is never far away. The landscape is predominantly agricultural, with some 18th-century but many 19th-century farmhouses and steadings, interspersed with small villages.

Kessock Bridge

Beaton

Cromarty Firth viaduct

Beaton

The re-routing of the A9 trunk road in the 1980s across the western end of the Black Isle over the splendid **Kessock Bridge**, 1983, Crouch & Hogg, with the consequent closure of the ferry between North and South Kessock, and the impressive **Cromarty Firth Viaduct**, 1980, Crouch & Hogg, has united the peninsula with its immediate hinterland. New housing for people who work in Inverness and who enjoy living in the Black Isle is the consequence. Cromarty is an outstanding example of an 18th-century Scottish burgh, important in national as well as local terms, with crowstepped houses, fishermen's cottages and historic parish church.

Redcastle, from 16th century
On a commanding mounded site at the head of the Beauly Firth, where the original castle of Edradour is believed to have been built by William the Lion in 1179. Roofless, red sandstone, roughly L-plan building with a square stair-tower in the angle; moulded corbel courses support the stair-tower parapet and angle corner turrets. It was once a magnificent castle, a balustraded viewing platform capping a five-storey stair-tower, with exuberant dormer windows and corbels. A plain wing was added in 1641, and remodelling by William Burn in 1840 included window enlargement and an arcaded loggia (demolished). From early 17th century the castle was owned by various branches of the Mackenzie family, passing to the Baillies of Dochfour in the 19th century.

Redcastle

Beaton

Fine range of **stables** in the parkland to rear of castle. One dated 1790 incorporates **carriage-houses** and is crowned with a central octagonal cupola; slightly later range at right angles with frontage defined by giant pilasters. **Greenhill**, early 19th century, was the Redcastle factor's house.

Redcastle Church (Killearnan Parish Church), rebuilt from 1800
Gothic, cruciform church incorporating early fabric on a site by the shore. A small recumbent medieval effigy is housed inside. The large 19th-century gabled **manse** beside the church enjoys panoramic views.
Coulmore, between Redcastle and North Kessock, is an early 19th-century, regularly fronted house with bowed outer bays, built of local red sandstone.

Top *Redcastle stables, 1790.*
Above *Redcastle Church (Killearnan Parish Church)*

1 **Kilcoy Castle**, *c.*1620
Red sandstone Z-plan castle occupying a commanding site overlooking the Beauly Firth. Angle turrets, circular bedroom tower, a plentiful supply of gun loops, armorials, pedimented dormers and corbelled turrets all embellish this handsome pile built by Alexander Mackenzie, fourth son of the Baron of Kintail. More Mackenzie coats of arms and initials are carved on the chimney mantel in the first-floor hall dated 1679. It was restored *c.*1900 by the Inverness architects Ross & Macbeth (who also designed the substantial rear wing). It is of considerable interest as an early and sympathetic restoration at a time when it was more fashionable to indulge in a complete re-build. Further restoration in 1968.

Above *Kilcoy Castle, turrets and bartizans.* Left *Kilcoy Castle*

Top *Kilmuir*. Above *Drynie House, Kilmuir, drawn by A & W Reid*

Kilmuir

Peaceful hamlet that contrasts with the urban sprawl of Inverness dominating the opposite shore of the firth. The roofless medieval **Kilmuir Church** with Y-traceried east window was converted in the 19th century into a burial mausoleum for the Grahams of Drynie, the site of whose burnt out house (1852, A & W Reid, Elgin) is indicated by a tree-lined avenue. **Croft Downie**, *c*.1830, gabled cottage orné with hood-moulded, lattice-paned windows overlooks the firth from the wooded hillside. **Drynie Mains** is a handsome 19th-century farmhouse.

MUNLOCHY

Munlochy strings out along the road at the head of Munlochy Bay, which is guarded by the mound of **Ormond Castle** (see p.16). **Munlochy Mains** is a villa-like, early 19th-century farmhouse. The spiky, late 19th-century **Knockbain Parish Church** (former Free Church) is one of a series of ecclesiastical buildings in the surrounding fertile valley. Its 18th-century T-plan predecessor was sited half a mile away with its **manse**, 1766, close by. Simple Gothic **Arpafeelie Episcopal Church**, 1810-16, remodelled 1876, Alexander Ross. His 1863 gabled former **parsonage** and **school** are a reminder of the strong local ties with that denomination.

Bogallan Free Church, 1888, John Rhind Chunky red sandstone building with lancet windows and square tower carrying squat faceted spire. The shell of the medieval **chapel** of **Allangrange** stands in the burial ground of the Frasers of that name.

Arpafeelie Episcopal Church

Old Allangrange

Old Allangrange, 1760

Handsome symmetrical two-storey traditional laird's house with Fraser coat of arms above its moulded doorpiece, and shaped wallhead gable. Its former low flanking wings were removed *c*.1900.

Allangrange House, enlarged 1907

W L Carruthers

Early 19th-century two-storey Allangrange House was elongated, retaining the original bowed outer wings, in Arts & Crafts manner carried out with sympathy. Tall **Roskill farmhouse** (1784) stands on the hill above the road to Avoch, its original proportions somewhat marred by later heightening.

Rosehaugh House (demolished), from 1893, William Flockhart

More a fairy-tale château than a Scottish mansion (the style influenced by Flockhart's Parisian architectural experience). Its inventive façade boasted a tall, square baronial tower and a wallhead encrusted with decorative dormers and shaped gables. The complex roofline formed a varied silhouette composed of tall chimney stacks, gables and spires. The interior was opulently appointed with rich, carved, panelled, plaster ceilings, handsome chimney-pieces. There was a swimming pool and tiled Turkish baths: the mansion was heated by a steam boiler blowing hot air through grilles and consuming a ton of coal a day doing so. Rosehaugh is still noteworthy for a rich collection of estate buildings in English Arts & Crafts manner unique in the Highlands: **farm steading**, 1812, of finest tooled ashlar (partially damaged

The wooded estate of Rosehaugh was once owned by the Mackenzies of Rosehaugh, of whom the best known is Sir George Mackenzie (1636-91), Lord Advocate during the reign of Charles II and founder of the Advocates' Library in Edinburgh in 1682 (opened in 1689). In the late 18th century it belonged to Sir Roderick Mackenzie of Scatwell who built a 'modern edifice' costing between £3000 and £4000. The Rosehaugh estate was bought and the old house re-modelled by James Fletcher, a native of Avoch with a fortune made in Liverpool, in 1864. James had been born James Jack, a common name in Avoch, but brought up in Moray where he married Isobel Fletcher and took her name. Their son, James Douglas, went on to expand the family empire and fortune with rubber and tea enterprises (there was a Rosehaugh tea plantation in Ceylon). He engulfed his father's solid square house, with a new mansion 1893-1903, designed by William Flockhart, a talented London-based Scottish architect, who had also studied in Paris. Many architectural fittings were salvaged before its demolition in 1959 to adorn homes throughout Scotland. James Douglas employed twenty-eight indoor servants and a dozen men in the vast gardens in addition to those on the estate and in the stables.

Top *Rosehaugh House, demolished 1959.* Middle *Rosehaugh laundry.* Above *Rosehaugh dairy*

Rosehaugh, glasshouses, 1907 (demolished)

by fire); **stables**, mid-19th century, with later additions in Flockhart gabled manner; a large walled garden, 1844, by C H J Smith, an Edinburgh landscape gardener; late 19th-century Tudor **electricity-generating house**; and a small, and now much overgrown, circular **burial ground** for James Douglas Fletcher, d.1927, and his wife Lilian, d.1955, designed by Sir Edwin Lutyens in 1928.

There is a fine trio of attractive English Arts & Crafts **estate buildings**, all *c*.1900, almost certainly by William Flockhart: **Gray's Cottage** with a pronounced front chimney pierced with small windows lighting an inglenook, timber studding and tiled mansard roof; the pebble-dashed **laundry** (originally the estate office) with more timber studding and tiled roof sweeping over a rustic porch; and the **dairy**, a long, low combination of cottage, dairy and byre, linked by a timber arcade in balanced asymmetry on a hillside site. The arcaded passage sheltered dairy staff circulating between the buildings and was wide enough to accommodate those bearing yokes with buckets.

Range of Hothouses erected at Rosehaugh, Ross-shire.

Burnthouse, close to Avoch village and aptly named, is all that is left of Avoch House (the home of Sir Alexander Mackenzie), burnt in 1833. It is one of a pair of crenellated service wings which flanked a three-window fronted house with a centre bowed porch.

AVOCH (pronounced Auch)
Ancient fishing village whose approach from the west is punctuated by the tall broached spire of the Gothic **Church of Scotland** to the north and the striking Italianate former **Free Church** at the south, both designed by Alexander Ross in 1872. The latter is now a house.

Sir Alexander Mackenzie (*c*.1755-1820) achieved fame as the explorer and trader in Canada after whom Mackenzie District and the Mackenzie River (which he discovered in 1789) are named.

Avoch village; site of Ormond Castle on Ormond Hill in background

RCAHMS

Hill House, 1820-2, Thomas Murison
Former manse beside the church, a simple sandstone house with masonry enlivened by dark cherry-pointing (fragments of stone pressed into the mortar), with 1845 additions by George Rhind. Former **Episcopal School**, 1853, Ross & Joass, Scottish Baronial, is inscribed *To the honour of Almighty God and as a Tribute to the memory of John Mackenzie Esq. of Bishopsgate, London, this institution was founded by a brother and sister, his two surviving children 1856*. Grandiose **gate piers** flanking the football ground, 1873, Alexander Ross, came from Rosehaugh House; the red sandstone **Station Hotel**, 1892, has its name proclaimed in elegant late 19th-century cast-iron lettering. Parallel **Alexander**, **George**, **John**, **James** and **Margaret Streets**, named probably after the Mackenzie families of Avoch House and Rosehaugh, are short, narrow roads

Alexander Ross, architect, inherited his father's Inverness practice in 1853 at the age of 19. *Not surprisingly, business was a little slack in the next few years but even so few architects have designed three churches, two manses and three schools before their twenty-fifth birthday ... In 1865 Ross was appointed architect for two very large and very expensive buildings, the Episcopal Cathedral at Inverness and the vast mansion of Duncraig Castle in Lochalsh ... [From then] Ross was firmly established ... He was the colossus among Highland architects ... in Ross are drawn together the threads of 19th-century Highland architecture, eclectic, practical and at times touching on genius, others of the drabbest, but always stamped with a force of personality* ... John Gifford, 1980

lined with cottages, many now enlarged with modern dormers. **Henrietta Street**, named after Lady Henrietta Wharton Mackenzie, an early 19th-century chatelaine of Rosehaugh, is a long terrace of simple whitewashed single-storey dwellings fronting the shore with the mound of **Castle Hill** (site of Ormond Castle) as a backdrop.

Church of Scotland, 1872, Alexander Ross Buttressed Gothic church with dormers in the arched base of the tall, faceted spire. It is flanked by columns with capitals decorated with realistic carved 'beasties' and foliage. The church stands on the site of an earlier church in a hillside burial ground overlooking village and Moray Firth. A rare pre-Reformation **Sacrament House** of c.1500, a small stone cupboard of unknown origin surmounted by a carving of a chalice, is built into the vestry wall. Interesting tombs in the burial ground, including that of Sir Alexander Mackenzie of Avoch House.

Top *Church of Scotland.*
Above *Sacrament House.*
Right *Carved beastie in porch.*
Right below *George Street*

A **Sacrament House** is an aumbry or mural cupboard in which the consecrated elements of bread and wine were retained for the use of the sick and dying. The one at Avoch came possibly from the **Chapel of Our Lady**, **Ormond Castle**, Avoch, the stronghold first of the de Moravia and then Douglas families, medieval Earls of Ormond with royal connections. Ormond was a courtyard castle of which only the foundations survive on **Castle** (or **Lady**) **Hill**. Alternatively the Sacrament House may have been installed by Abbot Robert Reid of Kinloss Abbey (see *The District of Moray* in this series) to which Avoch Church belonged in the Middle Ages. Reid repaired the church of Avoch during his incumbency at Kinloss (1504-28).

RCAHMS

FORTROSE

Fortrose crowds the clifftop above the Moray Firth, clustering around the ruins of its medieval cathedral and overlooking a small harbour bounded with red sandstone quays. The 18th-century houses and gardens flanking the cathedral green are the successors to those inhabited by the pre-Reformation cathedral clergy. Substantial late 19th-century villas stand in large gardens, developed after the town was linked to Inverness by a daily steamer. The 1980s and the construction of the Kessock Bridge have re-linked the area with Inverness, and new houses and bungalows now crowd the south-facing slope above the town, enjoying magnificent views across the firth. Fortrose is a delightful place in which to wander; through the dignified remains of the cathedral, the residential streets flanked with red sandstone walled gardens, or the cliffside paths leading to the shore and harbour.

Fortrose drawn by Captain John Slezer, 1694

Saint Boniface (otherwise Albanus Kiritinus or Cuiritan), thought to have been a 7th-century Irish monk, is said to have landed at **Chanonry Point** near Fortrose and to have established the first of various churches there and at Rosemarkie. It was not until the 13th century that the present cathedral at Fortrose was begun, the earliest remaining portion being the undercroft of the chapter house.

RCAHMS

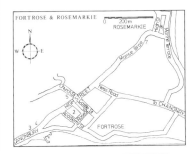

Top *Fortrose Cathedral, south aisle (L), Chapter House (R).*
Above *Bishop Fraser's tomb*

Nascentes Morimur Morienties Nascimur.
As Man as soon as Corn begins to Dye
So Death begins Mans Life of Immortality
Death Nature Time adieu all hail Eternity
Mans endless state must Be or Happiness or Woe
Tremendous their cause who Strive to show
Annihilation as a safer Creed
And Mankind a Mutum Necus Breed
Were not a Hereafter Mans Predestinated Lot
Mans Destiny would Be to Revel and to rot
Natures Shame and Foulest Blote.

Cryptic 18th-century inscription in Mackenzie of Coul burial enclosure, Fortrose Cathedral.

2 **Fortrose Cathedral**, 13th century
The spacious, yet intimate, Cathedral Square comes as a surprise after the narrow defile of **Fortrose High Street**. It was to this site that Bishop Robert (1214-49) moved from Rosemarkie to build a new cathedral. The choir, chancel and chapter house were finished probably by the end of the 13th century, the nave and south aisle following later. Excavations have revealed a building of approximately 185ft long and 25ft wide. Only the north choir range (combining Chapter House, Treasury and Sacristy) and the south aisle survive of this imposing and important cathedral constructed in local red sandstone. It is set in an open, tree-girt green bounded by the houses and gardens of **Cathedral Square**, **Academy Street**, **Rose Street** and **Union Street**.

The **Chapter House** has a mid-13th-century vaulted undercroft and first-floor chamber, reached by a later external forestair, used for burgh council meetings until 1939. A plaque over the door records that it was redecorated by General Sir Hector Munro KB MP in 1780.

The larger of the two ranges is the 14th-/early 15th-century **south aisle**: a long arcade of five pointed arches which once divided the aisle from the nave and resembles a giant loggia, its rib-vaulted interior lined with funerary monuments and lit from the south by empty windows once filled with tracery. A slender clock tower with later faceted spire abuts the wall.

The eastern portion is earliest, said to be the chantry chapel (devoted to singing masses for the dead) and burial aisle of Euphemia, Countess of Ross in her own right, who died in 1395. Three table tombs under arched canopies are alleged to be of Countess Euphemia and of two Bishops of Ross: Bishop Fraser (1498-1507) and Bishop Cairncross (1539-45). The south wall is dominated by a classical, columned and pilastered memorial erected c.1800 by Sir George Steuart Mackenzie of Coul (d.1848), to commemorate his father, Sir Alexander Mackenzie, 6th Baronet, a *Major-General in the Service of the Honble East India Company* who died in 1796 aged fifty-five. The polished sandstone monument, surmounted by an obelisk bearing the Mackenzie arms, is pierced in the centre by the entrance to a small mural chamber housing earlier Mackenzie of Coul grave slabs. A bas-relief carving of Father Time above the door is flanked on one side by a broken column and on the other by a ruined castle complete with a large medieval Y-traceried (?chapel) window. Does this represent the former Mackenzie seat at Coul, the predecessor of the handsome mansion erected there by Sir George in 1821? (see p.45-46).

Fortrose Cathedral, section, drawn by J J Joass

A plethora of marble tablets record and eulogise various members of the senior branch of the house of Mackenzie, the Earls of Seaforth. A late 17th-century plaque, notable for its bold strapwork, commemorates in Latin John Dunbar of Bennetsfield (now a farm between Fortrose and Munlochy), and his wife, Agnes Mackenzie.

Open to the public at all times

Bowed bay windows in Cathedral Square; No 7, The Town House, crenellated wallhead and tripartites (3-light windows)

Town House, 7 Cathedral Square, early 1800s

A charming town house, its bowed outer bays with three-light windows and crenellated wallhead very characteristic of homes built in the early 1800s by prosperous Ross-shire merchants, lawyers and smaller landowners. The delicate cast-iron porch is a later addition. The two-storey elevation of **8 Cathedral Square** (the rear of **32 High Street**) is fronted by a substantial projecting bowed wing. The Roman Catholic chapel of **St Peter and St Boniface** is housed in the former

Mackercher Hall, an Italianate volunteer drill hall designed by John Robertson in 1881.

Cathedral Green is bounded by **Union Street**, **Rose Street** and **Academy Street**, sites of earlier cathedral manses. Of these, the earliest surviving appears to be the range comprising **Angel** and **Rose Courts**, entered from Rose Street through a round-headed pend arch. Though of early 18th-century appearance they incorporate older fabric; Rose Court has an early 19th-century portico of striated cream and red sandstone, Angel Court an angel carved over the doorway. These two houses stand on the site of the pre-Reformation Deanery, the manse of the priest of Rosemarkie who was also Dean of Ross.

Academy Street is rich in interesting houses. At the High Street end **Flowerburn Cottage**, c.1838, displays a smart rear; the principal entrance is on the garden side approached by a flight of steps flanked by wide three-light windows. Tall, plain **Seaforth Place** is dated 1783 and adorned with fine scroll skew-puts.

Deanery, c.1730-40
Crowstepped with regular five-bay frontage enhanced by arched first-floor window. Later crenellated porch and rear drawing-room wing; the high rubble garden walls contain fragments of window jambs from earlier buildings. **Meadowbank**, a handsome two-storey house of c.1800 with porch, c.1830, is set in a walled garden entered through imposing gates and gate piers.

Episcopal Church of St Andrew, 1823-8
Substantially altered by Ross & Macbeth, 1891-1913, this Gothic buttressed and pinnacled church, with demi-octagonal apse at east balanced by a similar gabled baptistry at the west, stands on a clifftop site. Simple interior with good Victorian fittings.

Top *Academy Street.*
Middle *The Deanery.*
Above *St Andrew's Episcopal Church*

Fortrose Academy
Established in 1791, this building combines an amalgam of architectural styles reflecting a century of growth and expansion. The red sandstone range, 1890, by John Robertson, is entered through a round-headed main doorway at the base of a three-stage circular clock

*Fortrose Academy, marriage of old
and new architectural styles*

tower. It is linked to a glazed, three-storey rectangular classroom block designed in 1967 by M Kirkwood for Ross & Cromarty County Council. There are subsequent flat-roofed additions.

Craig-an-Ron, *c.*1900
White harled and gabled Arts & Crafts villa in the style of W L Carruthers with contrasting ashlar doorpiece, which enjoys and exploits a fine site overlooking the Moray Firth.

Local red sandstone 19th-century villas line **Canonbury Terrace**, many with fine cast-iron embellishment. **Craigdhu** has a bowed bay window canted at first-floor level and a decorative cast-iron balcony of exceptional size and quality.

3 **Canonbury House**, *c.*1865, ?Alexander Ross
An imposing villa entered through a porch decorated with stiff leaf-capitalled columns. The house is further embellished with shaped gables, cable-moulded detailing and a late Victorian conservatory.

4 **Kindeace Lodge**, *c.*1900, was almost certainly by William Flockhart. A sophisticated little red sandstone villa in interesting stylistic contrast with its more ponderous neighbours, built as the estate office for Rosehaugh, with contrasting pale dressings and some characteristic timber studding. A two-storey projecting wing has a shaped and ball-finialed gable and the steeply pitched tiled roof culminates with a tall, quoined chimney stack.

Kindeace Lodge, former Rosehaugh Estate Office; English Arts & Crafts in the Black Isle

Canonbury Terrace changes name to **High Street** where the shaft of the market cross stands in the pavement at the corner with

Academy Street. Gabled 19th-century **Woodside** has a re-cut 1740 datestone, apparently recording the date of the earlier rear portion of the house. **Nos 17-21**, 1869, John Rhind, form a charming terrace enhanced with Gothic detailing. High Street is tightly flanked by simple 18th- and 19th-century houses: **No 32** (8 Cathedral Square at rear), 1836, has a dignified symmetrical street frontage and decorative, dated scroll skew-puts at the wallhead. Opposite, the **Royal Hotel** turns the corner into **Cathedral Square** with aplomb and magpie paintwork; the date 1879 records alterations by Matthews & Lawrie. The Gothic **Parish Church**, 1895-8, John Robertson, former Free Church, has a gabled entry facing the street flanked by tower with spire and bowed gallery stairs.

Below Town Hall, former Parish Church, Fortrose. Bottom *Pictish cross slab, Groam House Museum, Rosemarkie*

5 **Town Hall**, **Church Street**, 1839
A dignified Gothic box with almost unaltered exterior, a former **Church of Scotland**; regularly spaced windows under heavy pointed-headed hood-moulds lightened by delicate, original intersecting astragals (glazing bars). The interior is lined with the Mackenzie of Seaforth portraits which once hung in Brahan Castle (demolished: see p.44), the ancestral home of the Mackenzies of Seaforth.

On the hillside above, early 19th-century **Platcock House**, with its symmetrical four-window frontage, is fronted by **Platcock Wynd** – retirement homes with dominant glazing by G R M Kennedy & Partners, 1987.

ROSEMARKIE
The narrow **High Street** is flanked with simple late 18th- and early 19th-century houses, some with gable ends abutting the road. The street is enlivened by the mid-19th-century chunky classical former **post office** with columned doorpiece. **Groam House**, c.1800, typical of many of its neighbours, has a plain two-storey, three-window frontage, with windows accentuated by coloured margins. Now a museum devoted principally to Pictish history, it includes the intricately carved Rosemarkie Cross slab amongst the exhibits.

6 **Parish Church**, 1821

The open site, with its panoramic view over
the Moray Firth and steps leading on to the
shore, is reached through a narrow lane
leading off the main thoroughfare, and comes
as a surprise from the cramped street.
Handsome if stilted Gothic building with
three-stage pinnacled tower (possibly yet
another of James Gillespie Graham's
provincial essays) entered through the base of
the tower. The crenellated minister's porch lies
in the centre of long south side, flanked by two
long windows; 1894 glazing in hood-moulded
windows. Interior re-cast and re-fitted to
design by John Robertson, 1894, fortunately
retaining the original handsome pulpit with
crown-shaped sounding board. A fine cross-
slab (now in Groam House Museum) confirms
the early nature of the site on which there
have been successive churches; that of St
Moluag in the mid-6th century, St Boniface's
monastery a century or so later, and then the
cathedral of Ross established by King David in
1125 which subsequently moved to Fortrose.

Parish Church, Rosemarkie

Below *Old Manse, Rosemarkie*
Bottom *Chanonry Lighthouse*

7 **Old Manse**, **Manse Brae**, 1833

Pedimented garden front, deep shouldered
gable chimney stacks and a regular rear
window pattern to impress the passers-by on
the road. It ranks as one of the finest manses
in the north and, in its time, was probably the
envy of neighbouring ministers.

CHANONRY

Chanonry Point pushes into the Moray Firth
marking the shortest sea crossing from the
south and the principal point of entry for
generations since St Boniface made his
landing in the 7th century. Boats plied
between Chanonry and a similar spit of land
opposite near **Ardersier**, occupied by **Fort
George** since 1747. The **pier** at Chanonry is
mid-18th-century as is the **Ferry House**,
probably a former inn providing shelter for
travellers. The fine, robust **lighthouse** with
its Egyptian-style **keepers' cottages**, was
designed by the Northern Lights engineer,
Alan Stevenson, in 1846. Note also the
substantial vaulted double-chambered
icehouse with pronounced gables; the turf

At **Chanonry Point** an inscribed stone (*above*) commemorates the supposed spot where Coinneach Odhar, the 17th-century Highland soothsayer (the **Brahan Seer**) who is said to have foretold the demise of the powerful Mackenzies of Seaforth of Brahan Castle, was burnt to death for his pains. Tradition tells that Isabella, 3rd Countess of Seaforth, pestered Coinneach as to why her husband lingered in Paris. So angry was she when told that he was dallying with a French lady that she ordered the seer's horrible death by burning in a barrel of tar on Chanonry Ness. Before he died, Coinneach prophesied that the last clan chief would follow his son to the grave, deaf and dumb, and that one of his daughters would kill the other. The last chief became deaf through illness and finally too weak to speak after seeing his four sons die, one after the other. His eldest daughter succeeded him: the carriage which she was driving near Brahan sustained an accident and her sister was killed. The place is marked by a memorial. See p.44.

Cromarty, view of town and firth

roofing, providing additional insulation, has been removed to reveal the vaulted rubble roofs; note chute for reception of ice (*above*). Former Black Isle Combination Poorhouse, 1859, by William Lawrie of Matthews & Lawrie, now **Ness House**, in Ness Road; this gabled institutional building has since been divided into flats.

CROMARTY

Formerly the capital of Cromarty-shire, Cromarty is one of the outstanding examples of an 18th-/early 19th-century Scottish burgh 'the jewel in the crown of Scottish vernacular architecture'. Situated at the entrance of the best deep-water firth in the north-east, it served as an entrepôt for seaborne goods and traffic from the 17th century to the early 19th. Although traditional sea traffic declined, and the burgh was bypassed by rail and road, the enfilade of drilling platforms stretching to the head of the firth like giant stepping-stones bears witness to the continuing value of this marine haven. Its narrow streets are lined with symmetrically fronted houses and cottages, some with sophisticated detailing, others quite plain. The earlier houses have steeply pitched roofs, their sharp profiles a reminder that the first quarter of the 18th

century experienced a cycle of poor weather: the steep roof relieved both earlier thatch and later slates of excessive rain.

The earliest landing place was at the east end of the town, now aptly named **The Causeway**. St Regulus Chapel and the former Castle were sited on the high ground above and the principal 18th-century buildings in The Causeway, **Burnside Place**, **Church Street** and **High Street**. The former **fishertown** meanders between Church Street and the shore.

Cromarty was owned by the Urquhart family, hereditary sheriffs of Cromarty, from mid-14th to mid-18th century. One of the best known members of the dynasty is Sir Thomas Urquhart (1611-60), soldier, writer and translator of Rabelais. The Urquharts were granted permission to build a tower or fortalice in 1470. This was a substantial L-plan tower-house to which a domestic range was added in 1632. In the early 1760s, Cromarty was purchased by Lord Elibank, to be sold again almost immediately to George Ross. He demolished the castle, building Cromarty House in its stead.

Cromarty owed its late 18th-century entrepreneurial prosperity to two people. The first, **George Ross** (c.1700-86), a native of Easter Ross, became a lawyer in Edinburgh and confidential clerk to Duncan Forbes of Culloden. He moved to London as an agent for army supplies as well as various Scottish bodies. He was a member of the Convention for Royal Burghs and the Board of Trustees for Manufactures. He purchased the Cromarty Estate in the 1760s (though the transaction was not finalised until 1772) and became MP for Cromarty-shire. In 1772 he demolished the 15th-century tower-house of the Urquharts, replacing it with the present Cromarty House. He poured his personal wealth into Cromarty, and his schemes were advanced both by personal contacts with the Establishment and his ability to work with local people.

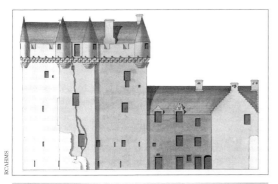

Top left Cromarty Castle in 1746, replaced thirty years later by Cromarty House (left)

8 **Cromarty House**, *c.*1772
Imposing classical mansion with wide, symmetrical five-window front, broad-pedimented and slightly advanced centre bay and set-back wings. Projecting bowed bay to the rear. Principal entrance is reached up a flight of steps, and the doorway is linked to flanking sidelights by a continuous open-pedimented cornice. The frontage is further embellished by a central first-floor Venetian window. Good interior plasterwork and architectural fittings. The architect is

William Forsyth (1722-88), Cromarty's other benefactor, originated from Moray before settling in Cromarty, where he became a successful merchant, trading with England and the Continent. He developed the flax and linen industry in the area, acted on behalf of local gentry, became a Justice of the Peace, a Superintendent of Roads for the County of Cromarty and an elder of the Church of Scotland.

Above *Cromarty House stables.*
Right *Cromarty House, detail of pediment and Venetian window*

unknown, although there are similarities with the contemporary **Culloden House** near Inverness and Dalvey near Forres (see *Moray* in this series).

Cromarty House is linked to the road by a **servants' tunnel**, contemporary with the house, enabling staff and tradesmen to come and go out of sight of the Laird and his guests in the *'lawn, garden, shrubbery and ornamental walks'*. Fine contemporary U-plan **stable** and **carriage house** with a lofty interior, the plaster vaulting borne on elegant wooden Tuscan columns. This will become part of the Cromarty outstation of Robert Gordon's Institute of Technology (RGIT), Aberdeen (see also the Old Brewery, Burnside Place).

St Regulus graveyard is the site of medieval chapel of which nothing survives, though the mound and partial moat (both natural) beg the

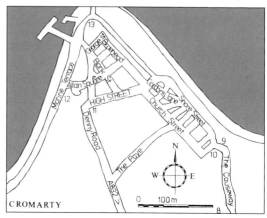

Cromarty is *a little town in a bottom, with one of the delicatest harbours reputed in all Europe, the tide coming in a great depth between two stately rocks (called the Sooters) through which the water passes in to a large bay....*
Thomas Tucker, 1665

question as to whether this was the site of an early fort.

The Causeway runs down to the shore and old landing place.

The Old Manse or Gardener's House, *c.*1690

T-plan house with early 18th-century additions, its crowstepped gables and steeply pitched roof characteristic of Cromarty architecture of this period. The moulded detailing to the principal doorway is a further refinement to this building which projects into the former **Cromarty House walled garden** stretching as far as Burnside. Restored in 1991 by the Scottish Historic Buildings Trust.

The Old Manse was built probably towards the end of the 17th century by John Laing, a merchant in Cromarty, the initials of whose son, also John, together with those of Margaret Clunes his wife, are carved above a ground-floor fireplace (they were married in 1721). John Laing the younger was a doctor (teacher of classics) at the 'Grammar School in the Canongate', presumably Edinburgh, and headmaster of Inverness Grammar School from 1709 to 1711. If the house was constructed by John Laing, senior, the additions appear consistent with having been made by his son. The house was sold about 1720 to John Reid, whose sea captain father drowned after sighting a mermaid (recounted by Hugh Miller). In the 1760s it was sold to Hugh Rose of Aitnoch, Cromarty Estate factor; subsequently it passed into that estate and at some period in its chequered history housed the gardener. In 1841 the house was used as a manse: sometime later Forsyth House, High Street, was purchased for that purpose.
(David Alston, Curator, Cromarty Courthouse)

The Old Manse, before and after restoration

Burnside Cottage

Clunes House, 1724
Crowstepped and white harled, with inscription JOHN CLUNES/ISSOBEL GRAHAM. **The Kennels**, mid-18th century, with its single-storey wings projecting to flank a small front court, incorporates some lintel fragments which may have come from the demolished Cromarty Castle.

9 **Burnside Place**: the diminutive **Burnside Cottage** is close by the shore and **Burnside** has a mural sundial at the wallhead.

10 **Old Brewery**, Burnside Place, established by 1776
One of George Ross's enterprises, this three-storey gabled building of two builds, with a five-window regular frontage, is now finding a new role as an outstation for Robert Gordon's Institute of Technology, Aberdeen. Converted by the Law & Dunbar-Nasmith Partnership, 1989, it has residential accommodation and, with the old Cromarty House stables, will ultimately provide studios and training facilities for home-based and overseas students with courses in social work, architectural and mechanical engineering.

Old Brewery

Church Street

Old Church (Cromarty East), from *c*.1700
Described as a *'true Presbyterian edifice'*, this
kirk is of exceptional interest in a Scottish as
well as a local context. White harled with free
stone margins, the long south elevation is lit
by two early 18th-century arched windows
with intersecting astragals lighting the central
pulpit and the bellcote in 1799. The doors were
blocked and re-placed by porches in 1848, the
small first-floor windows lighting the galleries.
The interior retains its traditional low-
ceilinged, galleried layout with pulpit (1915) in
the centre of the south wall. The Cromarty
aisle (or laird's loft) is grander than the other
two with a curved plaster ceiling, fine panelled
front and a funerary hatchment (diamond-
shaped plaque with armorial). Here the
spacious seating contrasts with the cramped
box pews in the north gallery (dated 1741 and
1788) and the west (or scholars') loft.
Interesting fittings in this unique church
include collection ladles, simple wooden hat
pegs projecting from the joists, and mural
memorials.

Top *(East) Church.* Above *Steeply
pitched gabled house, The Retreat,
Church Street*

Interior, Parish Church

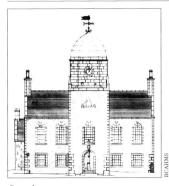

Courthouse

The Courthouse Clock has kept time for the people of Cromarty for over 200 years, almost without fault, and continues to do so. Until 1990, it was wound daily, the winder climbing the narrow staircase to the top of the tower and re-charging the mechanism with a sturdy key. Modernisation has meant that this task is now performed only every third day. The clock was made by John Ross of Tain in 1782; the bell of 1778 is slightly earlier with an enigmatic inscription SAN DIMAS CARACA ANO D 1778 – perhaps brought home by a Cromarty merchant venturer from Caracas, Venezuela? If so, this is a reminder that in its heyday, Cromarty men sailed the seven seas.

Courthouse, **Church Street**, 1771-3
The work of George Ross of Cromarty with funding from the Commissioners of the Annexed Estates (lands forfeited after the 1745 Rising) this handsome and imposing building represents burgh dignity and law enforcement. Two-storey symmetrical white-harled building with free stone margins, its robust projecting tower houses porch and stairwell, and is crowned with simple angle pinnacles and octagonal domed clock tower. Large, round-headed windows light the first-floor court room and there is a small **prison** to the rear by Thomas Brown (a noted prison architect), 1843. The **court room** remains unaltered with fittings of mid-19th-century date. The building is virtually unchanged although, its judiciary role long since removed elsewhere, it is finding a new use as an excellent and popular museum and visitors' centre. *Open throughout year*

Mercat Cross, ?1578
Placed in front of the **Courthouse** by George Ross in 1773 or 1778 (inscription indistinct), this simple shaft has a damaged cross finial and stands on a stepped base. The initials GR stand for George Ross, who moved it from in front of the former tolbooth in the **Causeway**. Though dated 1378 the cross is said to be from 1578, replacing its 14th-century predecessor.

Other public buildings in **Church Street** are the ugly **Hugh Miller Institute** (**Carnegie Library**), 1903-4, and the Gothic **Episcopal Church**, 1906, both designed by Ross & Macbeth. The tower intended for the church was never completed, though a local watercolour depicts the proposed design. Two pleasing stained-glass windows by Sir Ninian Comper (1932 and 1951), in which the sharp-eyed can find delicate strawberry plants; these were Comper's 'signature', a reminder that his father died giving strawberries to poor children.

Church Street, however, is mainly domestic in character. The **Retreat** dates from about 1700; early 18th-century **Albion House** with re-used 1713 marriage stone from a nearby demolished dwelling; **Buzancy**, mid/later 18th century; and **Wellington**

House dated 1829 – all dignified two-storey houses with regular frontages. The earlier houses have deep roll-moulded chimney copes, steeply pitched roofs and small windows, particularly at first-floor level where they are sited close to the wallhead.

Hugh Miller's Cottage, 1711

Low and thatched with small first-floor windows and crowstepped gables. The **sundial** in the small rear garden was carved by Miller. *National Trust for Scotland, open to public during summer months; guidebook available*

Miller House, *c.*1800, was built by Miller's sea captain father. The tall, regular-fronted two-storey house opens straight on to the street, the entrance reached by steps and the angles decorated with ashlar quoins.

Bellevue, *c.*1800

One of the larger houses in Church Street, this handsome red sandstone dwelling is set back from the road, the entrance flanked by fine gatepiers. Regular windows are somewhat marred by later glazing, and dormers are unsympathetic. Note how tall, three-storey **St Anne's**, *c.*1800, has the mortar joints of its squared red sandstone frontage galleted (or cherry-pointed) with fragments of contrasting dark slate. In the small garden of **Paye House**, late 18th century, lies the ruined gable of a cottage built by Hugh Miller for his aunt.

Top Paye House, Hugh Miller Cottage, Miller House (L-R). Above Hugh Miller Cottage

Hugh Miller (1802-56) was born in Cromarty, the son of a sea captain lost at sea when Hugh was only five. Miller served his time as a mason, but ill health forced him to give up that trade, and from 1835 to 1840 he worked at the Commercial Bank in Cromarty. He became a notable geologist, an author and a journalist – celebrated particularly for *The Old Red Sandstone*, and his garnering of oral tradition in *Scenes and Legends of the North of Scotland*. He corresponded with national figures such as Thomas Carlyle and Charles Darwin. Miller developed strong religious convictions. In 1840 he moved to Edinburgh as Editor of *The Witness*, the mouthpiece of the Evangelical Party and – in due course – of the Free Church of Scotland, formed in 1843 after the 'Disruption' had torn the Church of Scotland (the Auld Kirk) apart. This rift achieved considerable support in the Highlands. Miller, who suffered from visions and depression, committed suicide on Christmas Eve 1856.

Top *Hugh Miller monument.*
Above *Forsyth House, mercantile
prosperity with entry from High
Street flanked by imposing gate-piers*

*Mr Forsyth built for himself a neat
and very commodious house, which
at the time of its erection was
beyond comparison, the best in the
place and planted a large and very
fine garden. Both serve to show how
completely this merchant of the
eighteenth century anticipated the
improvements of the nineteenth.
There are not loftier nor better
proportioned rooms in the place,
larger windows, nor easier stairs;
and his garden is such as one would
satisfy an Englishman of the
present day. These are, perhaps, but
little matters:- they serve, however,
to show the taste and judgment of
the man.*
Hugh Miller, Memoir of William
Forsyth Esq (1839)

The Paye is a narrow lane winding upwards
from Church Street to the tall-columned
Hugh Miller Memorial, 1859, topped by the
statue carved by Handyside Ritchie. Here, too,
is the regularly fronted roofless Gaelic
Church, 1783, built by George Ross for the
many Gaelic speakers who came from
neighbouring parishes to work in Cromarty
(contrary to popular belief that they were from
the Highlands and Islands).

The junction of High Street and Church
Street is flanked by tall red sandstone No 1
Forsyth Street, 1808, and 2-4 Church
Street (of similar age) with a fine Edwardian
cast-iron shopfront.

Forsyth House, High Street, 1770-80
Confident and symmetrical two-storey house,
built for the entrepreneurial William Forsyth,
standing behind imposing cast-iron railings
and tall rusticated gate-piers. Note the fine
pinned (or Aberdeen bonded), red sandstone
frontage built over a basement from which a
tunnel runs under the road; how far this
tunnel ran originally is not known.

The rest of the High Street is lined mainly
with early 19th-century houses. Symmetrically
fronted Laurel House is dated 1828 and
initialled TB HS for the original owner and his
wife. Sydney House (No 12 High Street) has
a repainted date 1849 (probably erroneously,
for 1819 has been recorded) and the plain
exterior of No 8-10 High Street is enhanced
by an elegant doorpiece. The pedimented
Clydesdale Bank, 1876, was designed by
A & W Reid.

11 Townlands Barn, late 17th century
The laird's house of the small estate of
Sandielands; a regular five-bay front with
small first-floor windows, and quatrefoil vents
in the gables. When converted to a barn, a door
was slapped in the centre of the rear wall to
provide a through draught for the central
winnowing floor. Sandielands belonged to the
Revd Bernard Mackenzie, in 1678 the last
Episcopal minister of Cromarty. He was a
Mackenzie of Seaforth; the worn coat of arms
above the main entrance is said to be of that
family.

Ropeworks before conversion as housing

2 Hemp Works or **Ropeworks**, *c.*1775
The west side of **Cromarty** developed from the late 1700s, as a result mainly of increased activity generated by the hemp works established by George Ross, *c.*1775, and which introduced rope-making from *c.*1805. At its peak, these works employed 200 in-workers and over 600 out-workers. This two-storey range of local red sandstone with regular windows was constructed as a hollow square, with a fifth (long-demolished) block to the south. The seaward range was taken down in the 1970s. In the 1980s, it was converted by C R Williams (1984) and J McHardy (1989) of the District Council Architects to local authority housing with a restaurant in the east wing. It is a sympathetic and utilitarian use for a fine building no longer required for its original purpose.

Denny Road, **Allan Square**, **Bank Street**, **George Street** and **Duke Street**, all dating from turn of 1800s, are neat, regular two-storey, three-window houses flanking dignified, domestic streets. **Bank House**, **Bank Street**, has a well-tooled masonry frontage and good proportions; **George Street** is somewhat grander than its neighbours with larger houses, **Nos 3** and **5** linked by an arched pend and, like neighbouring **Reay House**, both have corniced entrances.

    Braehead fronts the shore overlooking the firth to the **North Souters** headland and
3 Nigg Bay. The **lighthouse** was designed by the engineer Alan Stevenson, 1846, one of a long line of lighthouse engineers drawn from the same family. The stumpy tower is flanked by Egyptian-style **keepers' houses**, similar to those at **Chanonry Point**. The 1825 **servants' cottage** was constructed to

Below Denny Road, oil rig in background. Bottom Neat artisans' houses in Barkly Street

accommodate the staff of the late 18th-century **Barkly House** (damaged by fire); **Alvara** and **Speybank Villa** link George and Duke Streets both physically and stylistically.

No 7 Braehead is adorned with a handsome date-stone depicting a tailor's iron and scissors dated 1727 with the initials of Kenneth Kemp and members of his family. **Links House (No 9)** has a fine glazed two-storey verandah on the garden front. The red and yellow sandstone **primary school** and **schoolhouse** by Andrew Maitland & Son, 1875-6, additions 1890 and 1904.

Cromarty fishertown lies between **Church Street** and **Shore Street**, linked to both by **Big Vennel** and **Gordon's Lane**. Randomly sited houses vary from small single-storey former fishermen's cottages to two-storey houses such as later 18th-century **Russell House** and early 19th-century **Seabank**.

Gordon's Lane

Above right *Big Vennel late 19th century*. Right *Big Vennel, 1991*

RESOLIS

A fertile parish lying immediately west of
Cromarty, bounded by the southern shore of
the Cromarty Firth, notable for three large
18th-century houses: Poyntzfield,
Braelangwell and Newhall. Resolis parish was
the charge of the Revd Donald Sage, author of
Memorabilia Domestica, the life and times of a
19th-century Highland minister. He 'came out'
at the Disruption in 1843 and lived for the rest
of his life at Jemimaville where he served the
Free Church. He is buried in Cullicudden
graveyard.

**The parishes of Kirkmichael
and Cullicudden** were combined
in 1662, the churches used on
alternate weeks. The site of the new
church in 1767 was a sunny incline,
Resolis or 'the place of light', and
that name gradually superseded
the old.

Jemimaville, from 1822, the principal village,
is a simple row of mainly 19th-century
cottages of which many are single-storey with
fine scroll skew-puts. Jemimaville was named
after Jemima, heiress wife of Sir George Gunn
Munro of Poyntzfield, with whose money it
was established. The **Old Manse**, *c.*1843
(former Free Church manse), stands out from
its neighbours with bowed outer bays linked
above the main door by oversailing piended
roof supported by two slender columns
reminiscent of the work of William Robertson
who built his own home, Ivy Cottage in Elgin,
in this style. (See *Moray* in this series.)
Robertson died in 1841, so possibly the house
had been built before 1843 and purchased by
the church for Sage, or earlier plans (perhaps
in possession of Fraser of Braelangwell (see
p.36)) came in handy when the manse was
needed immediately after the Disruption of
1843.

*Jemimaville, Old Free Church
Manse*

◄4 Poyntzfield, 1757
Originally called **Ardoch**, built and owned by
the Gordons of that name in the 1720s, altered
and enlarged in 1757, with yet later drawing
and dining rooms. In due course it was re-
named Poyntzfield after the wife of Sir George
Gunn Munro, the heiress daughter of Stephen
Poyntz of Cowdray Park, Sussex, whose money
was used to improve the estate after 1761. Low
wings flank the regular three-storey, five-
window frontage graced by a pediment perched
on the wallhead, a single number on each of
the four corbel-heads making up the date

*Poyntzfield; the shaped roof of the
rear prospect tower projects above
the roofline*

Braelangwell was the home of the Urquharts of that name. David Urquhart, 4th Laird of Braelangwell from 1776, married first Henrietta Gordon of Newhall, c.1785, whose family was associated with local industrial schemes: Newhall snuff mill (c.1750) and a series of flax, wool and corn-grinding mills at Gordonsmills, near Kirkmichael, of which one, dated 1796, survives. She may also have been responsible for the later 18th-century houses at Braelangwell and Newhall, both subsequently remodelled. Henrietta died in 1799 and David married Margaret Hunter in 1804. Their son David, born in 1805, was educated in France, Switzerland and Italy. This David Urquhart, a linguist and a diplomat, served for many years in the British Legation in Constantinople (Istanbul) where he earned the nickname 'English Bey', introducing Turkish baths to Great Britain. He approached the Pope with a plan for 'Universal Peace' which anticipated the League of Nations by a century, and served as MP for Stafford. He inherited Braelangwell in 1828 on the death of his half-brother Charles but scarcely lived there. Braelangwell was purchased by Lt-Gen Sir Hastings Fraser in 1839 who must have commissioned William Robertson to remodel the house; Fraser's kinsman, James Baillie Fraser of Reelig, had employed the same architect for the same task on his mansion of Moniack, later Reelig, in nearby Inverness-shire.

1757. An unusual feature is the small, off-centre, octagonal rear wallhead prospect tower with delightful swept ogee roof, after the style of that at **Foulis Castle**, also a Munro House (see p.56-7). Renovation in 1989 revealed features of the 1720s house. Carved stones dated 1673 lying in the courtyard may have come from the house in Church Street (site of Albion House and Wellington House) of Master Hugh Anderson, Minister of Cromarty, 1656-62, which was bought by Gordon of Ardoch. Aromatic commercial herb garden in the grounds. Little of **Ardoch** remains except the large barn or girnal (grain store) now converted as a house.

Beaton

15 **Braelangwell**, late 18th century (*above*)
Austere seven-window ashlar frontage defined by giant pilasters and Ionic-columned porch. The shallow bays advanced and recessed to give interest are the result of re-orientation and re-fronting to south by William Robertson between 1839 and 1844. Robertson died in 1841 and his work was completed by James Ross. Large courtyard steading, c.1800, at the rear.

RCAHMS

16 **Newhall**, 1805, James Smith (*left*)
Fine classical mansion with Doric portico and pedimented frontage graced by centre first-floor three-light window. An earlier house of 1730 incorporated to the rear. Richly carved Italian well-heads in the garden, and an unusual faceted sundial. The first **Newhall House** (ruinous by 1730) stood near the entrance gates. The estate has been in the same family since at least the 17th century, passing through both male and female lines. **Newhall Mains**, c.1830, is a handsome courtyard steading.

Ferryton Point girnal, mid 18th century
Recently converted as dwelling house, this long, low building was formerly the **Newhall Girnal**, the estate storehouse where rents in kind, such as grain or meal, were received from tenants, stored and in due course exported by sea to realise cash. In 1843, it was used as a preaching station by Donald Sage and his congregation who had 'come out' from the parish church in the Disruption.

Balblair Inn, 1820
Tall three-storey roadside hostelry to accommodate travellers, particularly those going to and from Invergordon by boat at **Balblair Ferry** (no longer in regular use). The long, roofless girnal close to the jetty is yet another example of buildings that accommodated the rich grain harvests of the Black Isle. A large vaulted single-chamber **icehouse** built into the slope at Newhall Point is a reminder of the formerly prosperous salmon-fishing industry here. **Kirkton Farm** nearby is a model early 19th-century agricultural complex dominated by a tall brick chimney stack which served the boiler-house generating power to motivate farm machinery, particularly mechanised threshing.

Resolis Church, 1767, James Boag, remodelled 1830
Plain rectangular church with unusual rear elevation, built against a slope to which it is linked by paired porches with cat-slide (sloping) roofs giving first-floor access to the gallery. Bell by George Watt of Edinburgh initialled DU HG 1787 (David Urquhart /Henrietta Gordon of Braelangwell). Traditional five-sided galleried interior with fine pulpit with ogee sounding board commemorating a former minister, the Revd Hector McPhail, minister of Resolis parish (1748-74).

The small medieval **Kirkmichael Church** stands in its burial ground by the shore near Balblair, the nave a mausoleum for the Shaw-Mackenzie family of Newhall. **Cullicudden burial ground**, between **Ferryton** and **Castle Craig**, is the site of Cullicudden Church, of which there are no remains.

Each proprietor, too, had his storehouse or girnal – a tall narrow building, the strong-box of the time, which at the Martinmas [11 Nov.] of every year was filled from gable to gable, with the grain rents paid him by his tenants, and the produce of his own farm.
Hugh Miller, *Memoir of William Forsyth Esq* (1839).

Below *Kirkton Farm*. Middle *Resolis Church, unusual rear gallery entrances exploiting slope.*
Bottom *Resolis Church pulpit*

Castle Craig

Castle Craig, 16th century
Tall, partially ruinous tower house perched above the shores of the Cromarty Firth. The decoratively corbelled and turreted wallhead is intact on the east side. Thought to have been erected by the Urquharts of Cromarty, and to have served, at times, as the residence of the Bishops of Ross.

17 **Old Logie & Urquhart Wester Church** is a ruin in the burial ground close to the shore; its successor, an austere rectangular **church** of 1795, stands to the west, remodelled 1894 by Ross & Macbeth. The neighbouring former **manse**, 1777, is fronted by a mid-19th-century addition whose horizontally glazed windows give style to an otherwise plain house.

Urquhart & **Ferintosh Free Church**, 1843; alterations, 1907, Thomas Munro, is a plain building with entry in base of later tower, capped by stumpy pinnacles and belfry. The church was established by Dr John Macdonald, the 'apostle of the north' and a moving force in the Disruption of 1843.

Urquhart and Ferintosh Free Church, with later tower

Tighnahinch, c.1830, is a pleasing farmhouse with three-light windows in first floor indicating that the parlour was originally
18 upstairs. At **Millbuie** there is a slender telescope-like **tower memorial** to Major-General Sir Hector Archibald Macdonald (1853-1903) – 'Fighting Mac' – a local crofter's son who excelled at the Battle of Omdurman in the Sudan.

Easter Ross

Much fertile farmland fringes the coastline and deep valleys run westward cutting into the hills and moors, some containing ancient tracks leading to the west coast. The principal towns are **Dingwall** in the south, at the crossroads of routes north and south, east and west, and **Tain** on the **Dornoch Firth** serving the northern areas. There are many small 18th- and 19th-century lairds' houses built by modest but prosperous landowners who were also involved either in commerce or the law – or both. The coastal parishes contain good agricultural land. The building of bridges and roads (particularly during the first two decades of the 19th century under the aegis of the Commission for Highland Roads and Bridges), the improvement of harbours and the advent of the railway in the second half of the 19th century encouraged both communication and development.

MUIR OF ORD & VICINITY

The site of the most important cattle fair in the north from 1820 to the end of the century and a trysting place for drovers from the glens north and west. The 'muir' on which the cattle were herded is now an industrial estate. The hillside flanking the village to the west is thickly scattered with crofts, established by 'mailers', or subsistence farmers, who carved smallholdings out of the barren uplands in the 18th and 19th centuries. Most of the cruck (wooden-framed) cottages have been altered or replaced but random layout is clearly visible.

Ord Distillery, founded 1838, has a pair of traditional pagoda-roofed kilns. **Ord House Hotel** is a pleasant 18th-century house with sympathetic later additions; **Ord Cottage** is ecclesiastical in character, hardly surprising since it was an 18th-century **Episcopal chapel** converted to domestic use by 1836 when superseded by the former **Episcopal chapel** at **Highfield**, now also a house.

Tomich House, *c.*1830, ?William Robertson
A symmetrical two-storey house with pilastered doorpiece and set-back wings, executed in well-tooled local red sandstone.

Below Ord Distillery, malt drying kiln with traditional pagoda roof. Middle *Ord Cottage, former Episcopal chapel.* Bottom *Tomich House, Muir of Ord*

Kilchrist chapel, nail-studded door

Kilchrist, Gilchrist or Cilliechrist (chapel of Christ) was *the scene of one of the bloodiest acts of Highland ferocity and revenge that history has recorded, commonly known as the Raid of Cilliechrist. In the early part of the 17th century, a party of Glengarry's men surprised a numerous body of the Mackenzies while assembled at prayer within the walls of Cilliechrist chapel, on a Sunday morning; shut them up within the building and then set fire to it; whilst the piper of the Macdonalds marched round the church, playing a pibroch, until the shrieks of the miserable victims were hushed in death. (Imperial Gazetteer of Scotland).* Needless to say the Mackenzies soon meted out revenge on the Macdonalds in like manner.

Tarradale Mains courtyard steading, *c.*1800, has a fine ogee-roofed doocot above the principal entrance crowned by salmon silhouette weathervane, indicating the former Tarradale involvement with commercial salmon fishing in the Beauly Firth. Much-altered **Tarradale House** is now a field studies centre for Aberdeen University.

19 **Kilchrist Chapel**, 17th century
Simple building incorporating earlier walls, mid-19th-century east window: arch-pointed doorway in the centre of the south front, and a pre-Reformation aumbry or cupboard for safe-keeping of Sacrament in north wall (see Avoch p.16 and Contin, p.44). Now a burial mausoleum for the Mackenzie Gillanders family of Highfield. Blocked gallery windows reveal alterations to internal layout for Presbyterian use after the Reformation, the steeply pitched roof probably a replacement after the 17th-century fire. The mean cast-iron apex finials substitute for a pair carved in 19th-century Gothic style, now lying in the surrounding burial ground.

Various driveways serving the **Highfield House** estate are identified by gate lodges: **North Lodge**, *c.*1840, with a romantic deep oversailing roof; **East Lodge**, 1867, with a steeply gabled roof with decorative bargeboards and cast-iron brattishing (ridge cresting), and L-plan **West Lodge**, 1874, designed probably by William Mackintosh. The **Dower House**, Highfield (formerly **The Cottage**), *c.*1800, is a long, low, white cottage orné with unusual circular chimney stacks.

Highfield House (demolished)

CONON BRIDGE

The village takes its name from the (demolished) five-arched **bridge** designed by Thomas Telford, 1806-9, which spanned the fast-flowing Conon River. The neat octagonal **tollhouse** was designed by Telford's chief assistant, Joseph Mitchell, in 1828; he also designed the **railway bridge** with its skewed alignment in 1860-2 for the Inverness & Ross-shire Railway. The early 19th-century **Conon Bridge Hotel** was established to welcome travellers in a village that straddles the road south. **Larchfield**, *c.*1910, is a pleasant house of the late Edwardian era, its doorway flanked by two-storey bowed bays, and piended roof decorated with simple finials typical of the period.

Conon House, 1790-9 (*below*)

Handsome, two-storey, white-painted mansion with Venetian windows in side elevation with later flanking bowed wings, *c.*1805, standing serenely in park-like setting near the Conon River. This is the home of the Mackenzies of Conon and Gairloch. Hugh Miller of Cromarty worked as an apprentice mason on the imposing **Mains steading**, 1822, built by Sir Hector Mackenzie, visible from the road with its centre-arched entrance under a three-stage belfry. A late 18th-century octagonal **doocot** stands on a knoll near the **Mains**.

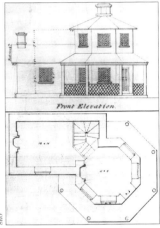

Top *Conon Bridge; elevation drawn by T Telford.* Middle *Toll House, drawn by J Mitchell.* Above *Larchfield*

Conon House: *One of the best houses I ever saw. He* [Sir Hector Mackenzie of Gairloch] *has continued to make those additions contributing to the neatness and regularity of the whole building, and to contain very elegant public rooms, besides other accommodation.*
George Steuart Mackenzie, *General Review of Agriculture for the County of Ross-shire* (1810)

Kinkell

Kinkell, 1594; restored 1969

Tall three-storey picturesque tower house on a commanding site overlooking **Conon Bridge**. White-harled with ashlar margins to the gun loops and ventilation slits in the vaulted ground floor and narrow windows above. The only doorway is in the base of the drum tower housing the winding newel staircase, the traditional, defendable entrance in a domestic house in which some defensive features linger. The large first-floor hall contains a wide segmental-headed hearth dated 1594. The house originally belonged to the Mackenzies of Gairloch, but degenerated in both status and maintenance before being restored as his home by the sculptor Gerald Laing in 1969. His sculpture decorates the garden where there is also his cottage studio.

Below *Former Seaforth Sanatorium, central block*. Bottom *Parish church, corniced doorway*

Seaforth Sanatorium, Maryburgh, 1907, Ross & Macbeth

'Erected and endowed for all time by Colonel James Alexander Francis Humberston Stewart-Mackenzie and his wife Mary Margaret for the treatment of Phthisis Patients belonging to the Counties of Ross and Cromarty.' This stone-built butterfly-plan sanatorium on a hillside above Maryburgh consists of large-windowed single-storey wings flanking the central two-storey administrative block. This sanatorium, no longer in use as such, was the model for others treating tuberculosis in Scotland.

URRAY
Urray Parish Church, 1780

Impressive rural parish church standing within its walled and tree-girt **burial ground**; minister's porch added in 1833. The 19th-century fashion for re-casting the interior to the east (instead of the traditional Presbyterian layout centring on the pulpit in the middle of the south wall) called for the insertion of large round-headed windows in the north wall in 1862 by Ross & Joass. Rather plain internal fittings; Communion Table designed by Ian Lindsay in 1938. **Old Urray**, the former manse, 1814 with subsequent additions, has a fine crowstepped **barn** of domestic proportions at the rear: this was the

Urray Parish Church

manse built in 1750 described not long after as 'the best in the synod'. It would have been conveniently close to the earlier church sited in the **Old Urray burial ground**.

Fairburn Tower, late 16th century
Tall pile of four rooms one above the other over vaulted ground floor fronted by early 17th-century stair-tower, on a commanding hilltop site overlooking Strath Conon and the coastal plain. Once home of the Mackenzies of Fairburn, the tower is now in the process of restoration by William A Cadell, Architect. The tower was superseded as a residence by **Fairburn House**, 1874-8, Wardrop & Reid, a handsome baronial mansion, now a nursing home, with a fine interior built by John Stirling of Fairburn on the neighbouring Muirton Estate. The **Gate Lodge** at **Aultgowrie**, also designed by Wardrop & Reid, 1877, sports dummy timber framing, carved bargeboards (wooded gable verges) and bears the initials JS for John Stirling.

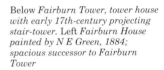

Below Fairburn Tower, tower house with early 17th-century projecting stair-tower. Left Fairburn House painted by N E Green, 1884; spacious successor to Fairburn Tower

Marybank Village flanks the crossroads leading from Fairburn to Moy; post office cum village shop, *c*.1870, the house front enhanced by a delicately glazed porch rescued from **Rosehaugh House**, near Avoch (see p.13). Shop and PO, once housing a tailor in the attic and coal merchant in the cellar, have served the community for over a century and continue this service despite crippling competition from supermarkets. The present shop interior is homely with some 1908 fittings.

The **Conon River** is bridged by the 14-span **Moy Bridge** with wrought-iron girders carried by cast-iron piers, 1894, Crouch & Hogg, Engineers, constructed by Cleveland Bridge Engineering Co. **Easter Moy**, a plain two-storey, three-window house, was built *c*.1800.

20

A squat octagonal **memorial** on a stepped base dated 1823 on the main road verge by an entrance to Brahan was erected to the Hon Caroline Mackenzie of Brahan, younger daughter of the last Earl of Seaforth, who was killed in a pony carriage accident – as foretold by the Brahan Seer (see p.24). **Brahan Castle** has been demolished; the fine **stable range** is now converted to house and estate office. The impressive **Mains farm square**, 1787-8, David Aitken, has central clock tower dated 1788.

Top *Marybank PO; delicately glazed porch windows salvaged from Rosehaugh House after demolition in 1959.* Above *Seaforth memorial, Brahan.* Right *Brahan Castle, late 19th-century photograph by George Washington Wilson*

Contin Church

CONTIN & STRATH CONON
Contin Church, 1796

Austere rectangular building incorporating medieval fragments, heightened in 1832: the south wall lit by two long windows flanking a projecting minister's porch. Alterations in 1908 revealed a small medieval pointed-headed sacrament house in the north wall in its original position. A finely carved tombstone in the church entrance is yet another reminder of the early Christian history of Contin and association with St Maelrubha in late 7th or early 8th century. The former **manse**, 1794, is gabled with later additions occupying with the church, an island site in the middle of the River Blackwater, reached by winding lane and bridge.

Contin Bridge, 1812-13, Thomas Telford
Handsome three-arched masonry bridge spanning the River Blackwater, now superseded by a new concrete structure carrying the A832.

Below *Contin Bridge*. Left *Coul House, 'octagon room' in centre, later bay window at right. Much of the 'horizontal glazing' has been removed*. Bottom *Ceiling in 'octagon room'*

Coul House, 1819-21,
Richard & Robert Dickson
Handsome gabled mansion of unusual plan, centred on two octagons with a demi-octagonal porch. The 'lying-pane' (horizontal) window glazing must be one of the earliest examples of this Scottish fashion in the Highlands. The central octagonal parlour is flanked by dining and drawing rooms, all with ornate plaster ceilings decorated with key pattern, anthemion (stylised honeysuckle) and acanthus leaves. Some of the building stone came from Cullicudden on the Black Isle, and was transported up the Dingwall canal and then by road to Coul; brick came from Brora, Sutherland, and slate from Easdale, Argyll, also probably by sea, canal and horse-drawn transport. Additions, 1860, Alexander Ross. The mansion is now a hotel reached by winding drive flanked by the **West Lodge**, 1819-21, R & R Dickson, who also designed a second 'Porter's Lodge', probably that on the Strathpeffer Road. **Mains of Coul** is a large hollow square dated 1795, the date-stone decorated with the Mackenzie crest. A portion of the building has been sympathetically

Coul was the seat of the influential Mackenzies of Coul. The present **Coul House** is the third on the site. The first may have been the castle depicted on the Mackenzie mausoleum in Fortrose Cathedral (see p.19), ruinous by 1746. Sir Alexander, a 'keen Agriculturist' who owned the estate between 1740-92, built the second, the timber coming from the estate. Sir Alexander's son, another Alexander, erected the large farm square in 1795. He rose to Major-General in the East India Company's service and was Provincial Commander-in-Chief of Bengal, 1790-2, restoring the family fortunes after almost a century of debt. His son, Sir George Steuart Mackenzie (1740-1848), lived in Edinburgh for some time and was a Fellow of the Royal Society of Edinburgh. His connections in that city account for his choice of architect for the new mansion he built in 1819-21. Like his grandfather, Sir George was also involved in agricultural improvements, and wrote *A General Review of the Agriculture of the Counties of Ross and Cromarty* (1810).

Coul House, West Lodge

Carnoch, 'Parliamentary' church

Carnoch, 'Parliamentary' manse

Kinlochluichart 'Parliamentary' church, 1827; 'T-plan' with later rear entry

converted as a home, *c.*1983. Leys of Coul housing scheme designed by Roan Rutherford will be developed from 1992.

Wooded **Strath Conon** stretches many miles west from **Contin**; **Scatwell House**, a multi-gabled shooting lodge incorporates an earlier house of the Mackenzies of Scatwell. Its 19th-century **Mains** is an imposing hollow square with tall tower over the entrance. **Milton** is an attractive village reached by an early 19th-century three-span bridge with causeway approach spanning the River Meig at **Bridgend**. The Gothic-detailed **Free Church**, 1892, is sited between Bridgend and Milton; the **FC Manse** was built and paid for in 1875 by Arthur Balfour, future Prime Minister and local landowner who *'encouraged the congregation'* with his support.

7 Strath Conon Church of Scotland, Carnoch, 1830, Thomas Telford
Standard 'Parliamentary' church with the paired centre windows flanked by outer doors, both with shallow Tudor-arched lintels. The church was funded by government money (see p.5) to serve a large and scattered congregation, many of whom followed the minister in 1843 when he seceded to join the newly established Free Church of Scotland. Contemporary (former) manse.

GARVE

Garve stands in the broad Blackwater valley, centre of a scatter of houses, farms and crofts through which pass the east/west road and railway. Besides the railway station there is an inn, school and diminutive walled burial ground, which was possibly the site of the pre-Reformation church of St Fionn. **Little Garve Bridge**, *c.*1762, probably Major Caulfield: a two-arched humped-back road bridge, carrying the (incomplete) military road on the north side of Loch Garve planned to link Contin with Poolewe.

22 Kinlochluichart Church, 1825, Thomas Telford
Some variation to the standard 'Parliamentary' design (see p.5); small windows replace paired doorways; the

entrance moved to rear and the interior re-cast. Delightful wooded setting overlooking Loch Luichart. Handsome **canopied tomb** to Louisa, Lady Ashburton (1827-1903). **Old manse**, also 1825 by Thomas Telford, but much altered.

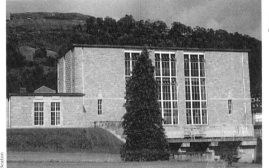

Left *Mossford Power Station.* Above *Kinlochluichart Church burial ground, Ashburton tomb*

Mossford Power Station, 1957, Shearer & Annand; engineers: Sir Alexander Gibb & Partners
Monumental Scottish Hydro-Electric generating station sited between hill and loch, the south front lit by three long windows. Associated terrace of red rubble **staff cottages**.

Strathpeffer *frequented by individuals of all ranks, from not only the County Ross and its immediate neighbourhood, but Caithness on the one hand and Aberdeen on the other*
Robert Chambers, *Pictures of Scotland* (1837)

STRATHPEFFER
Delightfully situated at the head of a broad and fertile valley of that name, Strathpeffer is Scotland's answer to the Bavarian watering place. The first published account of the qualities of the 'Castle Leod Waters' was given to the Royal Society, London, by Dr Donald Munro, FRS, in 1772 and by the end of the

Strathpeffer nestling in wooded valley

For over two centuries,
Strathpeffer has been known far
and wide as a place of healing,
where the natural Mineral Waters,
aided by life-giving mountain air
and restful atmosphere that
pervades the Spa, have triumphed
over disease and pain after
everything had failed; and the
health-giving properties of its
waters had a more than local
reputation for as long back beyond
that records are extant.
Undated Strathpeffer guidebook

Above *Old railway station with*
canopied platform supported by
graceful cast-iron columns. Right
Spa Cottage. Below *Kinnettas*
House. Bottom *Timaru*

century Strathpeffer had become a spa, initially only of local importance. It declined around 1810 but was revived from 1819 for a while by a Dr Thomas Mackenzie. In 1860 the Cromartie Estate (Castle Leod) commissioned the English architect George Devey, later to become eminent as a designer of country houses, to draw up a plan for the spa. None of Devey's house designs materialised but the layout of the roads up and down the wooded slopes owes much to him. There was further expansion with the coming of the Highland Railway in 1869. The opening of a branch line from Dingwall in 1885 brought visitors direct to Strathpeffer's canopied timber station; this influx in turn led to the construction of some large hotels and the development of the tourist trade, important then as now. The villas, sited on the wooded slopes above the village centre, reflect the architectural fashions in vogue during the growth of Strathpeffer, from simple symmetrically fronted houses of *c*.1800 to the exotic detailing of the late Victorian period.

Spa Cottage and the **White Lodge**, both *c*.1820, and **Kinnettas**, 1826-31, coincide with the genteelly elegant early 19th-century spa, with symmetrical proportions, simple harled masonry and ashlar margins. Mid-19th-century styles varied from solid homespun regularity of **Craigvar** to Italianate **Holly Lodge**. Exotic architectural decoration bloomed in the second half of the century with painted wooden verandahs, cast-iron finials and dummy timber framing. **Dunraven Lodge** and **Timaru** are richly balconied; **Holly Lodge** and **Dunichen** display a wealth of decorative cast-iron; the **Red House**, with its unusual tile-hanging, has an English flavour. The **Strathpeffer Hotel**, *c*.1800 onwards, has grown in size with the popularity of Strathpeffer.

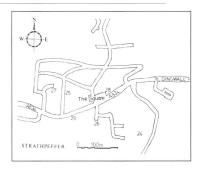

Ben Wyvis, 1879, additions 1884, W C Joass (possibly the original architect) Long, gabled grey rubble hotel with contrasting sandstone dressings and porte cochère. Frigidly grand dining room within. The most exotic is the **Highland Hotel**, 1909-11, by J Russell Burnett, which lives up to its name by dominating the village from an eminence, echoing a Bavarian schloss.

Nicholson Mackenzie Hospital, 1897, was established to provide treatment for those who could not afford the spa baths. Sadly the spa

and principal pump room were demolished in the 1950s, though a small **pump room**, *c*.1860, enlarged *c*.1890, survives.

Spa Pavilion, 1879-81, W C Joass Intended as a social focus in contrast to the medical and curative centre provided by the pump rooms, it has a central position in Strathpeffer. Applied timber detailing. Three pleasant **hexagonal buildings** designed by David Somerville in 1988 provide modern tourist facilities, including an exhibition centre. **Church of Scotland**, 1888, W C Joass, has a chunky Gothic gabled frontage. The **Free Church**, sited on the hillside above the Square, 1886, also W C Joass, contrasts dark grey rubble with sandstone dressings, the square tower capped by a faceted spire and the roof of banded dark and light slate.

Left *Pump room*. Middle *Highland Hotel and Spa Pavilion*. Above *The Square*

29 Episcopal Church of St Anne, 1890-3,
John Robertson
Gothic with buttressed aisle and drum
belltower, the lower portion forming the
entrance porch. Good interior fittings include
richly carved marble and alabaster altar and
reredos, marble pulpit and stained-glass
windows. Built in memory of Anne, Countess
of Cromartie in her own right and Duchess of
Sutherland by marriage (1829-88).

30 **Castle Leod**, *c*.1530-1910
Prominent on a rise in the vale of
Strathpeffer is ruby-red **Castle Leod**. There
is a massive carved pale sandstone lintel with
classical detailing dated 1616 over the
doorway, corbelled bartizans and wallhead
parapets with richly carved corbelling, built on
to original Z-plan tower by Sir Rorie
Mackenzie of Coigach, 1616. The wide dog-leg
staircase, 17th-century improvement to the
earlier tower, leads to the large hall with its
substantial fireplace. Fine untouched panelled
dining room. Various newel stairs wind their
ways upwards in the thickness of the walls to
the upper rooms: splendid turreted study at
the top. 19th-century rear wing in baronial
style (partly by D Bryce, 1854). Castle Leod is
surrounded by ancient trees and remains in
the Mackenzie family as the seat of the Earl of
Cromartie. **Gate lodge**, *c*.1840, with unusual
attenuated finialled skew-puts.

Right *Castle Leod*. Below *Ornate
armorial above main dooorway*

Until superseded by **Strathpeffer**, the centre
of the parish of **Fodderty** was in the middle of
the valley of the Peffery River; the present
burial ground identifies the site of the
original **parish church**. The white-harled
Fodderty Lodge, formerly the **manse** with
door lintel inscribed 17 MANSE OF FODDERTY 30
stands nearby.

*Kilvannie Manor Hotel, former
Fodderty Church of Scotland*

Kilvannie Manor Hotel, 1807
Former Fodderty Parish Church, converted to
house and later hotel, *c*.1900, after the centre
of worship had moved to Strathpeffer. The
ecclesiastical design of this red rubble
rectangular building has been cunningly
adapted for domestic use; the minister's porch
is the main entrance, round-headed doorways
have become French windows and gable
gallery stairs (1833) lead to the first floor. The
birdcage bellcote, originally at the church
gable apex, stands in the garden. Other houses
in the neighbourhood of note are **Beechwood**,
1794, which succeeded **Fodderty Lodge** as
manse; early-19th-century **Inchvanie**; and
Keppoch; *c*.1830, a pink-harled two-storey
house with bowed outer bays. **Millnain Mill**,
c.1830, now a dwelling house, retains a large
millwheel against one gable.

Fodderty, Beechwood, former manse

DINGWALL
A medieval market town situated at the head
of the Cromarty Firth; its name, of
Scandinavian origin, means Hill of Justice.

Dingwall, drawn by J Clark, 1824

DINGWALL

*... **though its trade** is still not very great, and though manufactures are conspicuous by their absence, Dingwall at least has a harbour ..... coasters had once to load and unload on the mud at low-water, their cargoes being carried along a bad road to and from the E end of the town. This inconvenience was remedied by shaping the lower reach of the Peffer into a regular canal, 2000 yards long, with two wharfs at which vessels of 9 feet draught can lie - such improvements being carried out in 1815-17 at a cost of £4365, of which £1786 was furnished by the Highlands road commissioners and £600 by the Convention of Burghs.* Francis H Groome, Ordnance Gazetteer of Scotland (1883)

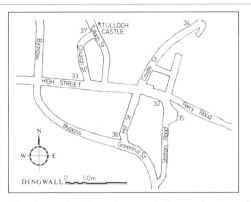

The town developed around the ancient castle of the Earls of Ross, of which only fragments remain in the garden of an 1821 house named **The Castle**, standing close to the old canal which linked it to the Cromarty Firth. A busy centre, particularly on market days when cattle floats crowd the mart area near **St Clement's Church**. The partially pedestrianised **High Street** retains many of its narrow passages and closes opening at right angles, some leading to sites cleared to serve as car parks. Dominant in the centre of the High Street is the **Tolbooth**. **Ross & Cromarty District Council Headquarters**, 1963, stand at the west end of the town, separated from the High Street by a ring road.

Above *Ross & Cromarty District HQ.*
Right *Tolbooth: tower, 1730; cupola, 1774; wings, 1905*

High Street
Heralded at the east by a cluster of good
buildings, the most important of which is the
32 handsome **Free Church**, 1867-70, John
Rhind, in French Gothic. Its buttressed walls
are pierced at gallery height by long traceried
windows breaking the wallhead within
gablets. A slender octagonal belfry caps the
square tower. In the grounds of the church
stands a plain shafted **memorial** to the Revd
John Kennedy (1819-84), an important figure
in the Free Church, and his wife (1819-96).

Free Church of Scotland

Classical **Royal Bank of Scotland**, 1906,
W C Joass, has a well-detailed frontage. The
Clydesdale Bank incorporates the 18th-
century **Park House** to contrast with the
modern banking hall. The **Hydro Board HQ**,

*Hydro Board HQ,
former National Bank*

1835-6, former National Bank of Scotland by
William Robertson, has a symmetrical
frontage and pilastered doorpiece, shorn of its
chimneys but expanded by a box-like glazed
extension at the rear. The **National Hotel**,
mid-19th century, is gabled with a decorative
cast-iron verandah linking outer wings; the
later 19th-century **Caledonian Hotel** turns
the corner where the High Street narrows.

33 **Tolbooth, High Street**, 1730
The most important building architecturally in
Dingwall now houses the **museum**. The 17th-
century solid, square tower is crowned by a
tall, graceful octagonal cupola, 1774, James
Boag, which still dominates the townscape.
The flanking two-storey gabled wings were
added in 1905 to a design by W C Joass.
Amongst other buildings of interest in a
sadly mutilated High Street is red rubble
Mansefield House with a pristine tiled

plaque dated 1897 commemorating the golden jubilee of Queen Victoria, complete with regal bust, burgh crest, monogram and turn-of-the-century floral border. The **Retreat**, 1791, additions 1825, is the former Church of Scotland **manse**.

No 64 High Street (McGregor's Close), 1786

Round-headed arched pend and wallhead gable identify a substantial town house once used as the Council Chamber. Meetings were held in an upper room with a coved ceiling.

Castle Street is positively ecumenical. The **Church of Scotland**, 1909, William Mackenzie, is the former United Free Church. **St James the Great Episcopal Church**, 1872, is the successor to two former churches of the denomination on the same site. The small 1806 chapel was replaced in 1852 by a Gothic building designed by the influential and prolific English architect, J L Pearson; when destroyed by fire, it was rebuilt close to the Pearson design by Alexander Ross. Further along the street stands the simple **Roman Catholic Church**. The quartet was completed by the first **Free Church** (1844), later the printing works of the *Ross-shire Journal* and then flatted housing, gutted by fire in 1990. A crenellated **folly** stands at the entrance to The **Castle**: though of earlier appearance, it is not indicated on the usually accurate Wood's map of 1822.

34 **The Castle**, 1821
Two-storey symmetrically fronted house with crenellated wallhead. It once sported a small rear wallhead prospect tower after the style of **Foulis Castle** (see p.56), **Poyntzfield** (see p.35) and **Balconie House**, near Evanton, now demolished. Overgrown fragments of **Old Dingwall Castle** are in the garden.

St James Street and **Achany Street**, linked to **Castle Street**, contain a harmonious residential group of late 19th-century villas.

35 The crowstepped and gabled **railway station**, 1886, has a cast-iron platform canopy.

Top *Jubilee tiled plaque.*
Above *Cromartie Obelisk*

Courthouse and **Police Station, Ferry Road**, 1864, Andrew Maitland
Imposing finialled gabled frontage, whose first-floor courtroom is lit by triple windows linked by continuous hoodmould. The earlier prison, 1842-3, at the rear was designed by the noted prison architect Thomas Brown.

36 **Park Cottage**, a once refined villa of *c*.1830 facing the by-pass, is in the style of William Robertson. Degraded, though still elegant, to a petrol station (Park Garage).

Above *Courthouse*. Left *St Clement's Church of Scotland*

37 **St Clement's Church**, 1799-1803, George Burn
Rectangular with Gothic windows, it is white harled with contrasting red sandstone margins (restoration in 1983 concealed the original red sandstone masonry cherry-pointing with dark chips). The pedimented north front supports a faceted **spire** and stands in a **walled burial ground** on the site of an earlier church. Grandiose **gate piers**, 1875-6, by W C Joass. Close to St Clement's, stranded in the centre of a car park, is a grey granite **obelisk** erected '*by George, First Earl of Cromartie, Lord Macleod and Castlehaven, who died at Tarbat House on 27th August 1714, in his 84th year*'. This originally marked the Earl's grave; the **obelisk** was re-sited and re-built in 1923.

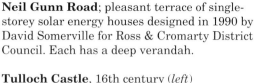

Neil Gunn Road; pleasant terrace of single-storey solar energy houses designed in 1990 by David Somerville for Ross & Cromarty District Council. Each has a deep verandah.

Tulloch Castle, 16th century (*left*) Originally the seat of the Bains, and then the Davidsons, it overlooks Dingwall from a rise on the north side of the town. The stolid two-storey tower has later regularised window pattern and tedious grey harling, relieved by a corbelled crenellated wallhead. Additions by Andrew Maitland in 1891; 1919 alterations by Sir Robert Lorimer who also designed the plaster ceiling in the first-floor hall. **Tulloch Mains**, 1774, is a large courtyard farm square entered through an archway. On the hill above the castle stand the remains of **Caisteal Corach**, a romantic castellated folly designed by Robert Adam in 1789-90. The **Macdonald Memorial Tower**, 1907, James Sandford Kay, provides an answering landmark on the Mitchell Hill to the south.

Above *Caisteal Corach, original drawing for folly.* Below *Mountgerald*

FOULIS

The south-facing slopes overlooking the Cromarty Firth offer favoured sites to many houses and farms. **Mountgerald**, *c.*1820, has bowed outer bays flanking the main entrance and a pedimented rear elevation showing a smart north front to the road. **Lemlair**, *c.*1875, probably W C Joass, displays a profusion of decorative cast-iron cresting and balustrades.

Foulis Castle, 1754-92 (*left*) Successor and namesake of an earlier castle destroyed by fire in mid-18th century, of which some walling and gun loops survive in the basement. A dignified white harled two-storey mansion with a profusion of smooth sandstone margins, the rear enclosed by a high walled courtyard. The long main south front is pedimented, the raised entrance approached by an elegant double stair while a tall canted bay window lights both return gables. At the back of the castle a projecting demi-octagonal tower rises above the ridge to contain an octagonal prospect room and library with a panoramic view of the Cromarty Firth (see

also Poyntzfield, p.35-6). Material salvaged from the fire includes the moulded treads of the graceful cantilevered staircase rising from the entrance stairhall.

KILTEARN
Ardullie Lodge, late 17th century
Small Munro house sited by the Cromarty Firth, steeply roofed and crowstepped. It incorporates several fine 17th-century date-stones decorated with an eagle, the crest of Clan Munro. The **Cromarty Firth Viaduct**, 1980, Crouch & Hogg, carries the A9 from the Black Isle over the firth to join the north shore opposite **Ardullie Lodge**. Long and low, the impressive quality of this viaduct is its length, curving its way over the water in a gentle crescent.

Foulis Ferry Renthouse (or **Girnal**), c.1730
Substantial three-storey storehouse, fronted by later forestair, in which the rents of Foulis Castle tenants were received and stored. There was an assembly area at the rear where goods

Top *Foulis Castle; rooftop view room with balcony rises above ridge to command a magnificent panorama.* Above *Foulis Castle; ornate cast-iron balustrade flanks entrance stair. Munro of Foulis armorial in pediment*

Foulis Ferry Renthouse

were unloaded from pack animals and carried into the girnal. The sheltered and gently shelving beach in the front of the store facilitated the loading of this agricultural cargo on to boats for export to realise cash in the urban markets of the south. Until the 1930s there was a ferry to Findon opposite; the ferryman's cottage is now a restaurant.

Kiltearn Church, 1790-1
Also on the coast, yet another, if roofless, reminder of the primacy of sea transport. There was an earlier building on this site as witness traces of a medieval window in the east gable of this T-plan church. The south wing accommodated the Foulis Castle Laird's Loft; with private access by forestair. Munro of Foulis burial enclosure dates from 1588. The glebe **steading** has been sympathetically converted to a house (*c.*1985).

Old Kiltearn Parish Church; the external stair led to the 'Laird's loft', the private pews of the Munros of Foulis Castle

EVANTON
The village was built from *c.*1800 onwards, superseding the earlier township at nearby Drummond. One of the earliest buildings in the village is the former **Secession Chapel** closing the head of the main street and converted as a dwellinghouse by John McHardy for Ross & Cromarty District Council in 1984. Built in the early 1800s (?James Smith, architect) it served a local congregation which seceded from the established 'auld kirk'. **Assynt House**, Glen Glass, 18th century, enriched and enlarged *c.*1840 by dummy bartizans and a wing.

Evanton former Secession (independent) Chapel, now flats

Novar House, 1720 onwards
Regularly fronted courtyard mansion with
later drawing- and dining-room wings, the
attic storey raised 1897. The late 18th-century
owner of Novar was General Sir Hector Munro
(1726-1805) who had served in India. It was he
who erected the **Fyrish Monument** on the
hilltop above Novar, a strange arcade of rubble
piers, some linked by pointed-headed arches
and said to represent the gates of Negapatam,
the scene of one of the General's military
victories. Other follies, somewhat less
dramatic, are scattered around the estate.
Fyrish House is an early 18th-century plain,
crowstepped house with later alterations,
standing not far from Novar.

Top *Novar House*. Above *Fyrish
Monument: a hilltop fantasy above
Novar*. Left *Alness High Street*

ALNESS
The village straddles the **Alness** or **Averon
River** and two parishes, **Alness** and
Rosskeen. Many simple 19th-century houses
line the long main street, both east and west of
the river crossed by a single-span bridge, 1811-
16, by Thomas Telford. The village expanded
greatly after the introduction of large
aluminium works in the 1970s at
Invergordon, an undertaking that closed a
decade later.

*Old Alness Church. Symmetrically
fronted 18th-century country parish
kirk. The long windows lit the
centrally placed pulpit and those in
the upper floor the gallery. Now
roofless and disused*

Old Parish Church, 1778-80 on an earlier
site, roofless, T-plan, stands on east side of the
village. The neighbouring **Old Manse**, 1791, is
dignified by an advanced and gabled centre
with doorway approached by flight of steps.
Cottage at rear with re-used chimney lintel
dated 1681.

Alness Parish Church, 1843
Unexciting red rubble former Free Church
with gable entry, square belfry with pyramidal
spire, and late 19th-century glazing; renovated
and enlarged, 1893. **Morvern Hotel**, 1843,
plain and square, is the former Free Church
manse.

Perrins Centre

Perrins Centre, **High Street**, 1903, probably
A Maitland & Sons
Interesting building in Arts & Crafts manner,
with good quality materials, an arcaded loggia
facing bowling green, tall coped chimney
stacks and elegant foliated lead finials. The
foundation stone was laid by Mrs Perrins of
Ardross Castle (see p.62).

Masonic Hall, formerly an Inverness church

Masonic Hall, **Invergordon Road**, 1863-4,
Alexander Ross
Small, rectangular and ecclesiastical in
character; decorated buttresses, traceried,
hood-moulded windows and stiff-leaf finials.
Originally built as Ness Bank United
Presbyterian Church at corner of Union and
Drummond Street, Inverness, it was re-erected
on its present site for its present use –
supervised possibly by Alexander Ross, himself
a keen freemason.

Teaninich House, 18th century and later
Older house refronted and encased in early
19th-century Adam castle style, it has a
symmetrical three-storey frontage with hood-
moulded windows and crenellated porch. Small
bartizans at battlemented wallhead. Fine
plasterwork in entrance stair-hall and an ogee-

Teaninich House

headed alcove on the stair landing to accommodate a grandfather clock. This was the seat of the Munros of Teaninich, farmers and soldiers; their estate **girnal** still stands (in poor condition) on the shore at **Alness Point**: a tall buttressed building erected in 1774 by Captain James Munro and his wife Margaret Mackenzie, whose faint initials and date can just be deciphered on the north-east gable.

Dalmore House, *c*.1890,
probably A Maitland & Sons
Large two-storey crowstepped gabled house of rambling 'butterfly plan' constructed in warm bullfaced sandstone. The mullioned windows and tall chimney stacks all indicate A Maitland of Tain as architect. Now a Church of Scotland Eventide home.

Teaninich House, elegant entrance hall

Alness Academy, 1976-7, William McQuirter for Highland Regional Council
Occupying a tree-lined green-field site, this school sports a projecting octagonal stairwell, a foil to the slightly squat two-storey range and added interest to the entrance front. A gracefully curved pedestrian road and railway fly-over is supported on brick piers.

Left *Dalmore House.*
Below *Alness Academy.*
Bottom *Struie, Easter Fearn Bridge*

STRUIE & ARDROSS

38 **Dal-Neich Bridge**, *c*.1815, Thomas Telford
Wide single-span bridge over the fast-flowing Alness River. The A836 Struie road from Alness to Bonar Bridge was a former drove road developed by the Commission for Highland Roads & Bridges between 1810-15. Two other Telford bridges on this road of the same period are the low twin-arched bridge at Strath Rory and the high single-span arch over the Easter Fearn Burn approached by a massive dry-stone causeway from the south.

Stittenham

39 **Stittenham**, 1835

The Duke and Duchess of Sutherland built their last staging post on the road north to Dunrobin near the drovers' stance in 1835, naming the inn **Stittenham** after their Yorkshire property. No longer an inn, the low gabled house has been somewhat altered by the blocking of the first-floor windows but the heavy masonry, crowsteps and diagonal chimney stacks identify the unmistakable Sutherland Estate building style. There were stables at the rear.

Ardross Castle, (*above*) re-modelled 1880-1, Alexander Ross

A modest Munro house enlarged by various owners until by 1880 it was bought by Charles William Dyson Perrins who had Ross add another thirty rooms in exaggerated baronial style. Drum and stair towers, crowsteps, turrets and caphouse, oriel and tall canted windows all have their place in this castellated confection, on its south-facing slope amid terraced gardens laid out by Edward White in 1910. Since Irish navvies provided the workforce, the village nearby has been called Dublin ever since. The **accommodation block** which housed these itinerant workers survives. Dyson Perrins also had built a Gothic **church** at **Ardross**, 1899, Ross & Macbeth, as a thanksgiving for the recovery of his wife from serious illness. Perrins stipulated that it was to be used by all denominations, unusual when the division between the Church of Scotland and the Free Church was rigid.

Charles William Dyson Perrins (1864-1958), who purchased Ardross Castle *c.*1880 and neighbouring Kildermorie, took over the management of Lea & Perrins, Worcestershire, from his father. Besides being a successful and wealthy business man (the Worcester sauce millionaire) he fulfilled many public duties in his own county and was a collector of pictures, manuscripts and early printed and wood cut books, many of which he gave to libraries and museums. He was a quiet, unassuming person. According to the poet Hugh MacDiarmid, who with his wife worked as servants for a short time at Ardross Castle, Perrins was *one of the most delightful and original little good-hearted freaks in Christendom.*

Kildermorie, at the head of **Strath Rusdale** midway between Easter and Wester Ross, is an upland fertile basin with a roofless **medieval church** (the church of St Mary – kil = church). It was a crofting township, cleared in 1792 to make way for a sheep farm and later a sporting estate. **Kildermorie Lodge** (incorporating an earlier farmhouse), with its gabled barge-boarded **keepers' houses**, **kennels**, **stables** and a pair of good game **larders**, 1860-90, is by A Maitland & Sons.

Wyvis Lodge, 1886
Incongruous 'stockbroker Tudor' shooting lodge, with stylised ribbon-pointed masonry, dummy concrete timber framing, and deep glazed verandahs enjoying a dramatic site on Loch Glass. Built for Walter Shoolbred, head of a London cabinet-making firm of that name (later Maples), the interior woodwork and much of the furniture were naturally of the best quality and fine workmanship. They were made in the firm's workshops in London, brought north by train to Alness, from whence they were transported up the glen by horse and cart to be offloaded on to a boat and finally ferried the length of Loch Glass.

INVERGORDON
Established by the Gordons of **Invergordon Castle**, which stood near the present **Mains Steading**, 1810. It achieved prosperity from early 19th century, becoming the major port on the Cromarty Firth. Large 18th- and 19th-century **warehouses** indicate past importance as a marine entrepôt, some of which have been converted to domestic or commercial use. Invergordon, a Royal Naval coaling station, became a permanent base in 1913, principally at the instigation of Admiral 'Jackie' Fisher. The **pier**, and the large **oil tanks** on high ground above the town, date from then. From 1913 until after the Second World War, Invergordon played an important role as a Fleet anchorage. Though the Naval presence has disappeared, Invergordon is headquarters of Cromarty Firth Port Authority. From 1968, British Aluminium works were established east of the town at **Ord**, creating a brief boom before closure a decade later.

Top *Wyvis Lodge*. Above *Game larder (one of two) and Lodge*

Invergordon Mutiny. *Through over-hasty decisions at the Admiralty and delay in explaining them, men of the fleet in harbour at Invergordon, awaiting naval exercises* 'heard of proposed reductions in pay of up to 25%'. *Such things, talked over in the large canteen in Invergordon on the evenings of the 13th and 14th* [September 1929], *when alternate watches of the crews had shore leave, gave rise to decisions for collective action ... Next day, 15 September, the men would refuse orders to fall in for work, to take the ships out of the harbour for exercises; this passive resistance was to begin on the battleships* Valiant *and* Rodney, *and to be shown by cheering, which would be the signal to the men on the other ships to follow suit. A moderate and loyal manifesto petitioning the Admiralty to review the reductions in pay was drawn up. All went according to plan. The admiral in charge cancelled all sailing orders ... [The Admiralty announced] on 21 September, that no reductions would exceed 10% ... Thirty-six 'ring-leaders' were dismissed the service, but with no charges brought against them; some officers were punished by premature retirement for having saved the Admiralty, by their moderation, from the savage consequences which might have followed on its own blunder.* Charles Loch Mowat, *Britain between the Wars, 1918-1940* (1955)

High Street

Long and broad, flanked by houses and shops. The Italianate former **Town Hall**, 1871, was converted in 1988 by Ross & Cromarty District Council to a community centre. Tall **Bank of Scotland**, 1856.

Shore Wynd, an 18th-century warehouse converted to housing *c*.1985, is the earliest building associated with the harbour. The **pier** is a relic of Royal Naval presence.

Cromarty Firth Port Authority HQ, *c*.1985, Thoms & Nairn

Modern harbourside architecture. The balconied seaward elevation is dominated by large windows from which to view the firth, and a projecting bowed and fully glazed stairwell floods the interior with light from sky and sea. This contrasts with the drab external cladding and tedious flat roof, alleviated by wide upturned eaves.

Railway Station, 1863, has a Jacobean shaped gable to cheer up an otherwise uninteresting frontage. It is worth venturing on to the platform to admire the fine cast-iron brackets supporting the glazed canopy.
Church of Scotland, 1859-60, Ross & Joass (former Free Church), terminates Castle Street, the slender spire soaring skywards, dominating the town.

British Alcan Smelter, 1968-73, D A Murray Ranks amongst the largest industrial works in the Highlands: an impressively massed complex, the physical reminder of a gross industrial miscalculation. The smelter went into full production in 1973, closing in 1982.

Kindeace House, *c*.1800

White harled with much use of contrasting golden ashlar sandstone dressings, and baronialised by Alexander Ross in 1869. The drive is flanked by a crowstepped **gate lodge**, *c*.1869, probably Alexander Ross, and fine decorative cast-iron railings. **Kincraig House Hotel**, dated 1800, had the same treatment but on rather more chunky lines by A Maitland & Sons in 1872. **Kincraig** was a

Mackenzie house; the Mackenzie stag and initials I MK M MK for John Mackenzie and Mary his wife are amongst the carved decorations on the original south entrance front. John was a Mackenzie of Redcastle; he inherited Kincraig in 1760 at the age of nine from a remote cousin. His wife was the daughter of the Revd Colin Mackenzie of Fodderty.

Newmore Castle, c.1600, a single-storey ruin with a multiplicity of gun loops, was replaced in 1875 by gaunt **Newmore House** designed by Alexander Ross.

Opposite: Top *High Street*. Middle *Cromarty Firth Port Authority HQ*. Below *Railway station, decorative cast-iron brackets support platform canopy*. Bottom *Church of Scotland with 140ft high spire*

Left *Old Rosskeen Church*. Below *Pulpit with elegant sounding board; steps and small doorway at rear lead to minister's room in tower*. Bottom *Munro of Newmore mortuary chapel*

Rosskeen Church, 1830-2, James Smith Imposing square church of original design built to accommodate 1200. Tall round-headed windows flank the central projecting tower on the south side contrasting with the small windows that light the building in a regular pattern elsewhere. Five-sided gallery and imposing pulpit. Neat Munro of Newmore mortuary chapel, dating probably from 1664: stepped 'mounting block' for horse-riders outside burial ground entrance. Disused.

40 **Balnagown Castle**, 14th century onwards Substantial Gothic wing, added c.1820 by James Gillespie Graham. Red stone with drum towers climbing up each angle, the ground floor softened by an arcaded loggia and pretty Regency porch. Varied slated roof profile, reflecting the many additions. Interestingly, according to MacGill (*Old Ross-shire*), in 1668 some of these roofs were covered with oak shingles. Richly appointed interior, the baronial first-floor hall (Trophy Room) with a

James Gillespie Graham had an extensive practice in Scotland, specialising in Gothic churches and castellated country houses ... the interiors [of country houses] often show a considerable facility in devising rich Gothic rooms. Howard Colvin, *Biographical Dictionary of British Architects, 1600-1840* (1978)

Top *Balnagown Castle*. Above
*Balnagown, large crowstepped barn,
fronted by later carriage house*

The first Laird of Balnagown
was reputed to be William, who
built the first castle in 1375. The
Rosses were extensive Ross-shire
landowners, and Admiral Sir John
Lockhart Ross of Balnagown
(d. 1790) became a well-known
agricultural improver. The property
remained in Ross hands until 1978.

magnificent chimneypiece of *c.*1700 decorated
with Ross armorials, a carved overmantle
dated 1680 re-used from Meikle Daan (see
p.82) and the ornate plasterwork and fittings
in the *c.*1820 dining room. In the policies, note
the great crowstepped **barn**, *c.*1700 (probably
the earliest and the largest in the Highlands,
now a games hall); an 18th-century long stable
range and the 18th-century high-arched **King
James Bridge** spanning the Balnagown
River. Mid-19th-century **Swiss Cottage** is
romantically sited above the river with lattice-
pane glazing and exaggeratedly deep eaves
supported by decorative brackets; a Ross-shire
interpretation of Switzerland taken from
J C Loudon's popular pattern-book, *An
Encyclopaedia of Cottage, Farm and Villa
Architecture* (1846) and the only building of its
kind in Highland Region.

Right *Swiss Cottage, Balnagown*.
Below *Design for Swiss Cottage by
J C Loudon, 1846*

Milton Village is centred pleasantly on a **green** with **market cross**, 1799, (*right*) an unpretentious ball-finialled shaft on a stepped base. The green is enclosed by late 18th- and 19th-century houses and cottages: amongst these the late 18th-century **Old Drovers' Inn** (now flatted dwellings) has a wallhead gablet and circular rear stairwell. In the 18th century Milton was an active centre of the local flax linen industry. The **mill**, dated 1858, was re-built after fire in 1900; it is the successor to a long line of mills at 'Milntoun'.

Kilmuir Easter Parish Church, 1798 Large, plain with long arched windows filled with later glazing. Altered internally, 1906, by John Robertson. Linked to the east wall is a gabled portion of an earlier church with a circular tower; the pepperpot stone belfry pierced by lucarnes (tiny gabled vents). A date-stone is boldly inscribed 'Beigit 1616' with the initials GMR and the Munro eagle's head.

41 **Tarbat House**, 1787, James McLeran Imposing mansion which incorporates part of **New Tarbat House** built by Sir George Mackenzie, Viscount Tarbat and 1st Earl of Cromartie in late 17th century on site of an earlier castle. Austerely classical three-storey, seven-bay frontage with tall first-floor windows and regular rear elevation lit by a centre Venetian window. Suitably classical **stable** range. Sadly and needlessly neglected for many years.

Middle *Drovers' Inn.* Above *Kilmuir Easter Church, tower, 1616, with portion of old church now burial mausoleum.* Left *Tarbat House*

Tarbat House *is quite plain outside. Within are some handsome rooms. A great deal of space has been taken up by the architect having indulged himself in displaying wide landing spaces, and a spacious staircase. These are extremely pleasant during summer months but are hardly suited to our long and dreary winters. The rooms are elegantly proportioned, and there is a fine view of Cromarty from the windows of the principal rooms.* George Steuart Mackenzie, 1810

Top *East Lodge, Kildary, designed 1889, Andrew Maitland & Sons, with mock timber framing.*
Middle *Scotsburn House.*
Above *Old Logie Easter Church, 1818-20, style of James Gillespie Graham, architect (demolished)*

Nigg is one of the mensal
[mensal = with glebe land providing food] *churches that belonged to the bishopric of Ross. Behind the church is still to be seen the foundation of a large house above 90 ft in length, which goes under the name of the Bishop's House, though not the place of his constance residence; and the hill ... is, in old charters of the lands of the parish, called the Bishop's Forest. One of the vaults of the house remained entire in the year 1727.*
Statistical Account of Scotland, (1793)

Arabella and **Shandwick (Old** and **New**) are lesser houses representing the tradition in Easter Ross of small but prosperous estates. **Arabella**, *c*.1800, its centre a projecting bowed bay with crenellated wallhead, was named after the first wife of Hugh Rose of Glastullich who bought the estate, and built or improved the house. **Old Shandwick**, 1790-1805, '*a handsome mansion*', was built by Sir George Cockburn Ross of Berwickshire who succeeded in 1790: handsome indeed, even in its present dilapidated state, with centre crenellated bowed bay, Venetian windows and the remains of an elegant cantilevered staircase. Replaced by **New Shandwick**, *c*.1900, faintly echoing the style of its predecessor.

Scotsburn House, *c*.1800-10
Unpretentious, two-storey house on a gently sloping site overlooking the Cromarty Firth; of pleasing proportions and constructed of warm yellow-brown sandstone, it is said to have been built by Simon Mackenzie.

Crowstepped **Marybank**, mid 18th-century, **Kelton House**, 1780, and **Logie House**, 1855, are all former manses. The present **Logie Easter Parish Church**, 1903-5, A Maitland & Sons, was the former United Free Church.

NIGG, FEARN & TARBAT
Nigg, **Fearn** and **Tarbat** parishes span the eastern seaboard of Easter Ross, stretching between the **Cromarty** and **Dornoch Firths**.

Nigg Parish Church, 1727 (*below*)
This long, low, venerable church retains its 18th-century character, probably incorporating the old church of 1626; rear wing 1786.

Alterations in 1864 by A Maitland were sympathetic to the building. It is a good example of a simple Highland rural church standing in its burial ground, wonderfully sheltered by trees. The **Nigg stone**, a Pictish cross-slab, is housed within the church. **Nigg** has connections with pre-Reformation bishops and their lands. **Nigg House**, *c.*1800, with slightly later drawing room wing at the rear, is on the site of the former 'Bishop's House' and incorporates a re-used date-stone of 1702 and probably earlier fabric. There is documentary reference to *'the manor place, mansion, garden, moothill ...'* etc; the site around church and Nigg House all indicate earlier settlement.

RCAHMS

Nigg Church Hall, 1844, ?James Smith
Former Free Church sited close to the shore in simple red rubble building lit by traceried windows. Dignified by a delightful projecting four-stage tower fronting the entrance gable with porch in the base. The slim tower changes shape at each stage, from square through octagonal to circular, capped by a diminutive pagoda roof supporting a weathervane.

Beaton

Old Nigg Manse, 1808, is plain and crowstepped, and 1840 projecting wing creating an L-plan. **Nigg Hotel**, incorporating a girnal (estate storehouse) dated 1712, stands on the beach and the former ferry site to Cromarty on the opposite shore.

Bayfield House, *c.*1790 (*below*)
Symmetrical three storeys with long first-floor windows indicating the principal rooms, set back wings and substantial paired hipped

Historic Scotland

Top *Nigg: cross slab in parish church. A superb example of Pictish carving; the interlace decoration reveals elongated animals while at the apex St Paul and St Anthony share a loaf of bread held by a raven.* Middle *Nigg Church, local blacksmith's door handle.* Above *Nigg Church Hall (former Free Church)*

Beaton

wallhead chimney stacks. An earlier house was incorporated in the farm steading. Rambling **Pitcalzean** may be earlier but overlaid with many later additions and a re-cast frontage; the novelist Eric Linklater and his family lived here from 1946 to 1971. **Chapelhill Church**, 1871-2, by Alexander Ross, is Gothic with a square tower, deriving its name from the Secession (breakaway) chapel that formerly stood on the site. At **Ankerville**, three dormered cottages, *c*.1900, have been fitted into a former 18th-century warehouse, the crowstepped gables the only architectural feature to draw attention to the building's earlier character.

Ankerville Cottages

Historic Scotland

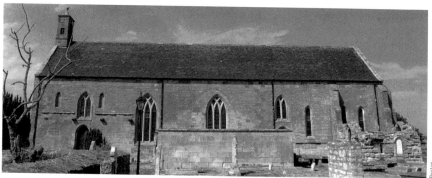

Beaton

Fearn Abbey

Fearn Abbey, from 1238; rebuilt 1771 Large, rectangular gaunt kirk with mid 18th-century birdcage bellcote. Gable lancets, blocked Venetian windows and later large Gothic windows with tracery. Two roofless medieval chapels project from south elevation and one from north. First established near **Edderton** in 1221 by Farquhar, Earl of Ross, under an abbot from Whithorn (Premonstratensian order), and moved to the present site on richer land *c*.1238. Rebuilding was carried on between 1338 and 1372. Used as the parish church after the Reformation the roof fell in in 1742, killing about fifty worshippers. Fearn Abbey was re-built in 1771, largely at the instigation of Admiral Sir John Bruce Lockhart Ross of Balnagown, whose handsome memorial is at the rear of the church, decorated with a square rigged ship in full sail (designed by John Baxter II). Former **manse**, 1825, stands close by, now divided into three dwellings.

Cliff House, Cadboll, 1984, Andrew Thoms

Thoms

Fearn and **Hill of Fearn**, two settlements close to one another, have characteristic single-storey cottages of unusual construction found elsewhere in the neighbourhood, with clay or clay and boulder walls, and small off-centre ridge chimney stacks. The cottages at **Inver**, formerly a fishing village, are often longer than those in Fearn: some have (or had) a central passage from front to rear, and three rooms with fireplaces. Although many have been modernised, the position of the small ridge chimney identifies them and the local vernacular building tradition.

Above *Fearn, local vernacular cottage with rectangular clay 'lums' at left gable end and ridge; corrugated iron roof replaces former thatch*

Fearn Railway Station, 1864, Joseph Mitchell
A neat two-storey station and station-house with single-storey wings. The platform canopy is supported by slender cast-iron columns.

Cadboll Castle, 16th century
Vaulted ruin, superseded by the small crowstepped gabled **Cadboll House** *c.*1700 (now greatly enlarged). The property belonged to the Macleods of Cadboll, whose 19th-century factor, Crawford Ross, has been immortalised as a silhouette windvane mounted on the mid-17th-century lectern **doocot**.

42 **Rockfield Castle** or **Little Tarrel**, a late 16th-century petite crowstepped towerhouse, restored *c.*1982 by A Gracie, has a worn re-used window cill inscribed 'Litil Terrel 155?'.

Top *Cadboll House.* Above *Cadboll doocot.* Left and below *Rockfield Castle (Little Tarrel) before and after restoration c.1982*

Geanies was a Macleod property. The last Macleod of Geanies was Donald Macleod, Sheriff of Ross from 1774 to 1837. After his death the following year, the property was bought by Kenneth Murray, a member of a Tain merchant and banking family and a noted agriculturist, whose memorial stands in the High Street. Of the house, Sir George Mackenzie noted in 1810 how its external appearance showed how it had been built at different times without any fixed plan but that *there is a great deal of elegant and comfortable accommodation within.*

Geanies House, variously 18th- and 19th-centuries with the *de rigueur* Easter Ross projecting bowed and crenellated drawing and dining room wing of 1820-30. The wooded grounds contain a delightful clifftop **gazebo** of *c.*1800 incorporating a fine re-used marriage lintel dated 1760.

Right *Geanies House.*
Below *Ballone Castle*

43 **Ballone Castle**, later 16th century
Splendidly opulent (if roofless) castle standing on a natural coastal terrace overlooking the Moray Firth. It has the standard Z-plan form, with round bedroom tower (with private staircase) and principal stair within a square tower in the opposite corner. Kitchens and cellars on the ground floor open off a transverse service corridor (a late 16th-century development) rendering the apartments above that much more spacious. The upper storeys, the dressed stone turrets and the corbelling would, when set against the harling of the rest, have rendered Ballone magnificent. This 'fortalice of Easter Tarbat' was first a stronghold of the Dunbars of Tarbat and then the Mackenzies, abandoned by the latter family in favour of Tarbat House, Milton, in the late 17th century (see p.67). After centuries of neglect, **Ballone** is being restored by Lachlan Stewart, architect, for himself.

Balintore

Beaton

PORTMAHOMACK

The **pier** at Portmahomack, built at the end of the 17th century by Sir George Mackenzie, 1st Earl of Cromartie, is almost certainly incorporated in the present simple harbour, 1813-16, by Thomas Telford. It is fronted by Lord Cromartie's 17th-century, low, massively solid, two-storey **warehouse** (*above*) and another of three storeys dated 1779 with regular fenestration and apex ball finials. Both had collection yards at the rear. Houses, many of 18th- and 19th-century date but with altered windows and later dormers, follow the curve of the bay. There is a delightful cast-iron **fountain** (*right*) with a cherub under a domed canopy dated 1877 (probably MacFarlane of Glasgow) commemorating, in both Gaelic and English, the introduction of 'gravitation water' (piped water) to Portmahomack (*below*).

Beaton

Sir George Mackenzie, Viscount Tarbat and 1st Earl of Cromartie (1630-1714), Highlander, Edinburgh lawyer and holder of high legal office under six sovereigns including the posts of Lord of Session and Lord Justice Clerk. Mackenzie exploited his lands in Easter Ross, improved the agriculture, built water-mills at Milntoun (Milton) and New Tarbat, and developed the harbour at Portmahomack (first called Castlehaven, a name which never stuck) from when he exported grain and other produce to realise cash. Mackenzie's legal salary was not large and it was sometimes up to seven years in arrears! Besides New Tarbat House at Milton he built Royston House (now Caroline Park) near Granton, Edinburgh, conveniently near the port where his ships arrived from Easter Ross.

Beaton

Old Tarbat Parish Church, 1756

Small, white-harled T-plan disused church on a rise above the village which incorporates a pre-Reformation vaulted crypt below the eastern end. Although the dedication to Bishop (later St) Colmon is medieval, there has been a church on this site since 1255. The church is notable for its unusual squat ogee tooled sandstone **belfry**, each face punctuated by

Old Tarbat Parish Church

diminutive lucarnes (gabled vents). The belfry appears to date from *c*.late 17th century; the bell is dated 1764. Handsome 17th-century mural memorials in the church, and some fine **burial enclosures** and **monuments** in the surrounding walled **burial ground**. Of note amongst these is the Macleod of Geanies enclosure against the west wall of the church and the handsome Thomas Dingwall and Hector Mackenzie monument with flanking columns and side panels. The plain and gabled **Old Manse**, 1808, stands close by the church. The Gothic **Free Church**, 1892-3, A Maitland & Son, is next to its plain but dignified manse of 1845. **Tarbat Ness Lighthouse**, 1830, by Robert Stevenson (heightened 1892), is identified for ships at sea by two red-painted bands that encircle the tower. Egyptian-style **keepers' cottages**, 1830, also R Stevenson, the first in the long dynasty of Stevenson lighthouse engineers.

Dingwall and Mackenzie monument, Old Tarbat burial ground

Tarbat Ness Lighthouse

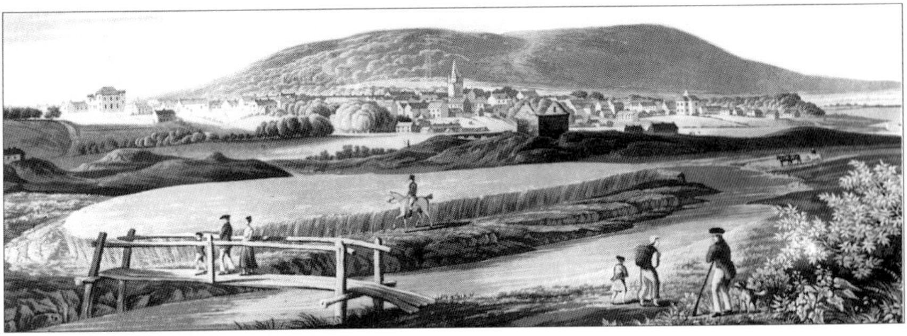

RCAHMS

Tain, drawn by John Clark, 1828

TAIN

A centre of medieval pilgrimage to the remains of St Duthac (or Duthus), originally to the 13th-century ruined chapel on the links on the outskirts. The town is sited at a junction of land routes from south, east and west; also from the north by the **Meikle Ferry** across the **Dornoch Firth** to link with Sutherland, an ancient ferry route now spanned by a viaduct (1991) carrying the A9 northwards. It was 'erected' (created) royal burgh in 1588, and developed in random fashion round the **Collegiate Church**, the **Tolbooth** and the **High Street**. From 1827, a planned residential area was feued by Macleod of Geanies as principal landowner, which included **Knockbreck**, **Geanies** and **Ankerville Streets**. There was no local architect of note until Andrew Maitland established himself in the town in 1842. Most of Tain's surviving houses date from the 18th century onwards and many streets are domestic in character, lined with simple two-storey houses or 19th-century villas.

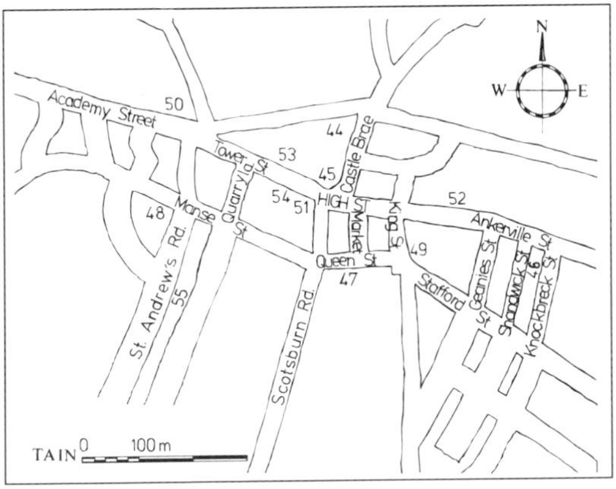

St Duthus [or Duthac] *was an ancient and favourite place of pilgrimage, and the old church having been consumed, this new one would, after its erection, be doubtless the celebrated shrine to which James IV and V made their pilgrimages. The former king is believed to have gone there every season for at least twenty years, as part of the penance he performed in connection with his father's death. He visited St Duthus in 1513, before his last fatal expedition, which closed with the Battle of Flodden. In 1527 James V made the pilgrimage of St Duthus barefoot, a memento of which event is preserved in the name of the 'King's Causeway', by which a road near the town is known.*
D MacGibbon & T Ross, 1896

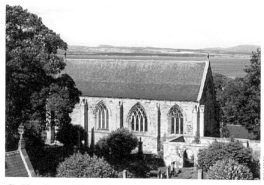

Right *Collegiate Church*. Top *16th-century oak pulpit*. Above *interior photographed by the Victorian photographer, George Washington Wilson*. Below *Tain Tolbooth*

44 Collegiate Church, 14th and 15th centuries
Compact, rectangular buttressed building with pointed-headed doorway at south-west lit by large traceried windows filled with fine Victorian stained-glass, save for the rear, where narrow lancets sufficed in the north elevation exposed to the sea and gales. Note the pointed and trefoiled triple sedilia and piscina in the south wall, and the elaborate 16th-century oak **pulpit** (restored later 19th century), said to have been presented to Tain by Regent Moray as a mark of his appreciation of 'the zeal of the town in the cause of the Reformation'. Mural tablets to local worthies line the interior. The origin of the small roofless building in the surrounding **burial ground** is unknown.

The Collegiate Church was used as the parish church until superseded in 1815; after being restored in 1849-82 by Robert Matheson and again in 1896 by Hippolyte J Blanc, it was set aside for memorial purposes. *Open to the public.* **Museum**, housed in the former caretaker's cottage, 1884-5, by A Maitland & Sons, is *open during summer months*.

45 Tain Tolbooth, 1706-33, Alexander Stronach
The original Tolbooth was demolished after serious storm damage in 1703, although its bell, 1630, by the well-known Flemish bell-founder Michael Burgerhuys, together with an inscribed fragment of 1631, survive. The massive two-storey square tower of the Tolbooth has angle bartizans and is topped by a squat, conical, stone steeple crowned with a weathercock. The round-arched ground-floor entrance was created in 1848-9 when the

tower was linked to the baronial **Courthouse**, 1848-9, by Thomas Brown (which probably incorporates 1840s prison cells by A & W Reid). Clock-faces and retaining parapet added in 1877.

The **Mercat Cross**, restored 1895, is a simple octagonal shaft capped by lion rampant, which stands in the angle between Tolbooth entrance and Courthouse.

46 **St Duthac Church**, 1811-15, James Smith
Now the **Duthac Centre**, this building succeeded the **Collegiate Church** as the burgh centre of worship. Square 'four-poster Gothic', the angles of the building are clasped by dummy crenellated angle turrets and the south front lit by two large traceried Gothic windows with thick wooden mullions. Hood-moulded windows in other elevations with intersecting tracery or blind openings. It is degraded by alterations necessitated by its new role as a public hall, such as the later porch and crowstepped public conveniences.

47 **Parish Church**, 1891-2, A Maitland & Sons
Handsome, Italianate former Free Church, the tall open campanile dominates the roofscape in opposition to the ancient Tolbooth steeple. Giant fluted pilasters clasped to the pedimented frontage; there is an imposing and well-lit galleried interior. **St Andrew's**
48 **Episcopal Church**, **Manse Street**, 1887, Ross & Macbeth, is Early English with a high-pitched roof. Good woodwork within by the woodcarver Robert Thompson of Kilburn, Yorkshire, whose hallmark was a mouse which the observant visitor will spot in various parts of the building. Neighbouring gabled **parsonage** of 1898 by Alexander Ross.

Andrew Maitland (1802-94), a native of Keith, Banffshire, who trained in Edinburgh, appears to have been an assistant to William Robertson, Elgin, and probably first came to Ross-shire to supervise alterations to Braelangwell, Resolis (see p.36), from 1839. He established himself in Tain in 1842 soon after Robertson's death. Maitland was a good draughtsman, very hard-working and inventive. The French Gothic **Royal Hotel** (1870), the Italianate **Parish Church** (1891-2) and Tudor gabled shops in High Street, Tain, testify to his variation of style and quality of work. The firm became A Maitland & Sons after James and Andrew Maitland joined their father.

Parish Church

RC Church, Cameron Road, 1985

Duthac House

49 **Associated Presbyterian Church**, 1839
(former Secession Church), King Street, is
notable for its beautifully tooled masonry
frontage, the original symmetry marred by the
blocking of two doorways. In marked contrast,
the modern **RC Church of St Vincent de
Paul, Cameron Road**, 1985, Thoms & Nairn,
is a spacious L-plan building combining church
and presbytery. With spindly free-standing
campanile, pale Skye chip finish and concrete
tiled roof, the design is practical but bland.

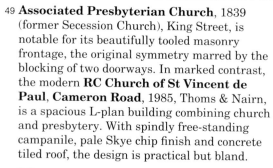

50 **Duthac House**, 1803-13, James Smith
The former Tain Academy, this fine building
was once considered '*one of Scotland's
handsomest and chastest erections in the north
of Scotland*'. End bays project slightly, with
three-light windows. The entrance is dignified
with a pilastered doorway and there is further
dignity in the large first-floor D-shaped room
(former Assembly Hall) reached by a
processional staircase. It has found a new role
as a home for the elderly. Ancillary buildings
now house special and nursery schools – the
infants sometimes grandchildren of the
residents.

*Tain, dummy timber framing in
High Street*

Tain Royal Academy, from 1968, replacing
the former academy
Extensively glazed and harled geometric
blocks designed and constructed in two phases:
1968-9, by George Smith of Ross & Cromarty
County Council; 1975-6, Thomas Forbes of
Highland Regional Council.

High Street, terminated at the west by the
51 French Gothic **Royal Hotel**, 1872, A Maitland
& Sons, is flanked by buildings of various
architectural styles. **Nos 1-25** High Street,

early 19th century, are all executed in well-tooled sandstone, many with original ground-floor shopfronts and three-light (tripartite) windows to the first floor. These windows, characterised by narrow side-lights flanking a large centre window, were much in vogue in Easter Ross during the first half of the 19th century for lighting drawing and dining rooms. Neat piended dormers to attic rooms. On the north side of the street, **Nos 14-16**, late 19th century, have thin dummy timber framing whereas there is French Renaissance detailing to **William Ross, Jeweller (Nos 18-22)** – designed in 1897 for a craftsman of that name (his home over the shop) by A Maitland & Sons. The **District Council Office**, 1828, former Commercial Bank, is a tall L-plan building with unusual blocked eaves cornice.

52 Fine crocketed **monument**, 1879, by Laurence Beveridge, sculptor T S Burnett, both Edinburgh, commemorates Kenneth Murray of Geanies (1825-76; see p.72): a mini 'Scott Monument' adorning Tain High Street.

The former arcaded **Market** in Market Street, mid 19th century, now a series of small shops. **Clydesdale Bank**, 1878, A Maitland & Sons, is notable for the extensive use of decorative cast-iron work at wallhead and ridge.

53 **Bank of Scotland, Tower Street**, 1845, George Angus
Two-storey classical bank (formerly British Linen Bank) with a regular frontage and centre pilastered doorway. Originally, it had twelve-pane glazing as revealed by the 'blind' gable windows. Sympathetic banking hall.

54 The Renaissance **Town Hall**, 1874-5, A Maitland & Sons, is disused and down at heel. **Tower Gardens**, c.1820-30 (adjoining the 1902 pair of houses of that name by Thomas Munro), is a single-storey cottage with shallow piended roof and horizontal glazing.

55 **New Manse, St Andrew's Road**, 1822-4, ?James Smith
A grandiose house with pedimented front and giant angle pilasters, which replaced the plain, regularly fronted **Manse House**, 1800. Neither serves as a manse any longer.

Below *District Council Offices, former Commercial Bank.* Middle *Clydesdale Bank, formerly North of Scotland Bank.* Bottom *Murray memorial, High Street*

Quarry Lane, local authority housing, 1989, David Somerville for Ross & Cromarty District Council
Sensitive scheme of single-storey dwellings, two of them incorporating existing high rubble walling. Generous windows and glazed porches, dark slated roofs.

Below 10 Knockbreck Street; wide panelled pilasters, shallow advanced centre bay and moulded window mullions suggest a design by William Robertson of Elgin (1786-1841). Right Mayfield

No 10 Knockbreck Street, c.1830-40, a symmetrical two-storey house with panelled gianted angle pilasters, has thick moulded window mullions and piended roof with projecting eaves. **Mayfield**, Morangie Road, is on the same lines. Both these two houses are in the manner of William Robertson who is known to have worked in Easter Ross. Did Robertson work in Tain? Or were his designs and style brought to Tain by his former assistant, Andrew Maitland, who settled there.

Typical later 19th-century Victorian villas include **Craigdarroch**, c.1875, and **Mansefield Hotel**, 1902, both in **Scotsburn Road**, and **Lauderdale** in **Morangie Road**.

Knockbreck House; the bowed outer bays are characteristic of Easter Ross

High Mills; pair former woollen mills. The two water wheels exploited a single lade (leet) to provide water power

TAIN ENVIRONS

There are some smaller rural houses of quality in Tain's hinterland. **Knockbreck House**, c.1820, has characteristic bowed outer bays, pilastered portico and corniced wallhead; internal fittings beautifully detailed. **Hartfield**, c.1830, has a recessed centre bay and pilastered doorpiece. Early 19th-century **Aldie Mill** was in use until the 1970s. The unusual pair of woollen mills at **High Mills** of the same period are sited one above the other, each with a waterwheel motivated by the single lade. **Glenmorangie**, converted from a brewery in 1842, is a well-established whisky distillery with traditional buildings. The spirit stills are unusually tall, which may be a factor in the production of its distinctive flavour.

Glenmorangie Distillery

EDDERTON

Edderton Bay is sheltered by a long spit of land terminating at the ferry point of the **Meikle Ferry**, the traditional crossing place from Tain in the south and **Dornoch** and **Sutherland** in the north, linked by a road viaduct opened in the summer of 1991 by HM The Queen Mother. Joint design engineers were Crouch, Hogg, Waterman & Ove Arup.

Old Edderton Church, 1743

Long, low, disused building surrounded by a burial ground in which there is a carved cross slab. Despite the small 19th-century dormers, old Edderton Church has never lost its original mid-18th-century character and, unusually, has scarcely been altered. The simple, low building with small square-headed windows, the plain doorways in each outer bay with plank doors and original blacksmith-wrought handles, set in its drystone-walled burial

Old Edderton Church standing within walled burial ground by the shore

ground, is a rare survival. A roofless burial aisle of 1657, possibly the chancel of an earlier church, abuts the east gable. Crenellated Gothic enclosure at the west, *c.*1802, houses the mural memorials of the Baillies of **Rosehall**, **Sutherland**. The church was superseded by the new church in the centre of the village in 1842, only to be re-used a year later to serve newly established Free Church congregation.

Edderton Church of Scotland

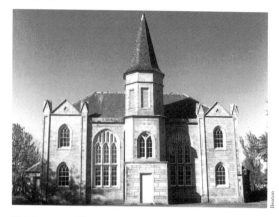

Edderton Church of Scotland, 1842, ?James Smith
Imposing square, self-confident, red sandstone building with a tower projecting from the centre of the south elevation, capped by a faceted bellcast spire and flanked by large Gothic windows. The minister's entrance is in the base of the tower, and porches for the congregation abut each gable. An inserted ceiling hides the five-sided gallery; the original sounding board, decorated with delicate pilaster detailing, projects over a later pulpit. There must have been a local source for these testers – a similar fine example was in the **Free Church**, 1844, at neighbouring **Lower Gledfield**, **Ardgay** (removed 1988-9); there is also a pretty example at **Loth**, 1823, both Sutherland.

Two churches call for two manses. **Old Manse**, 1799 with additions 1838 and 1855, is gabled and roughly cruciform. **Eastburn House**, 1844 (former Free Church manse), has a plain frontage enlivened by a corniced

doorway. **Edderton Mains**, 1819, by local
mason Nicholas Vass is a simple house
forming an L-plan. Late 19th-century **Fearn
Lodge** is a large gabled shooting lodge; **Mid
Fearn** a Victorian cottage with rustic porch
and canted dormers; **Wester Fearn** a simple
farmhouse *c*.1800. **Balblair Distillery**,
established 1790, rebuilt on new site 1895. It
has a traditional malt kiln with pagoda-like
ventilator.

Top *Balblair Distillery*. Above *Mid
Fearn, Victorian rustic porch*

Meikle Daan, 1680

Plain two-storey house in the uplands above
the village. The lintel is initialled AM MF for
Alexander Munro and his wife Margaret
Forrest. There is evidence of an earlier
staircase, while an elaborately carved
chimney-mantel of 1680 has been removed to
Balnagown Castle (see p.65-6).

Wester Ross

The rugged coastline of Wester Ross with its
magnificent scenery differs greatly from the
greener, softer and more fertile Easter Ross.
The only road communication between the two
sides of the District is from Dingwall through
Garve although, in the past, use was made of
the many routes through glens, now the
domain of walkers. Land ownership and family
ties once linked both sides of Ross and
Cromarty more than today. Settlements and
crofting townships fringe the coastline; small
areas of fertile land are often occupied by a
laird's house (now usually a shooting lodge),
generally the former homes of members of the
multifarious Mackenzie family. Sea
communication carried not only people,
livestock and goods, but also architectural

ULLAPOOL

fashion, materials and local building traditions. There are some fine 18th-century lairds' houses with features peculiar to Wester Ross and, in the agricultural context, long ventilated cruck (timber-framed) barns for the storage of hay and unthreshed corn.

Of the thousands who throng its streets every year, there can be few who fail to notice how distinctively the village has been planned. The bustling activity of Ullapool today may not have quite fulfilled the Directors' dreams, but its variety would surely not have displeased those men of vision who laid the foundation of the British Fisheries Society nearly 200 years ago.
Jean Dunlop, *The British Fisheries Society, 1786-1893* (1978)

The Governor, Deputy Governor, and Directors of the British Society for extending the Fisheries and improving the Sea Coasts of the Kingdom ... having agreed for the purchase of about 1500 acres at Ullapool on Loch Broom ... are willing to receive proposals for the erection of the following buildings: a warehouse ... a pier on that part of the southern beach at Ullapool ... as shall be best adapted for the purpose ... an Inn ....
Aberdeen Journal, March & April 1788

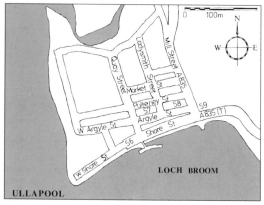

ULLAPOOL

ULLAPOOL

Occupying a panoramic site jutting out into **Loch Broom**, Ullapool was one of three west coast sites chosen by the British Fisheries Society in the late 18th century for the establishment of fishing villages (the others being **Lochbay**, **Skye**, and **Tobermory**, **Mull**). Approached by road from the east, white houses along the curve of the shore are reflected in the waters of Loch Broom ringed by hills sheltering the bay while westwards, the open sea is dotted with the **Summer Isles**. The village was laid out on a grid pattern in 1788, the Society providing the public buildings necessary for the herring fishing-pier, Customs House in which to store salt for fish curing (then subject to duty) and an inn.

Ullapool

The grid pattern remains evident in the five parallel roads of **Shore**, **Argyle**, **Pulteney**, **Market** and **Customs House Streets**, bisected by **Quay** and **Ladysmith Streets**. It afforded regular plots for houses which were feued and built by individual settlers.

The local fishing failed intermittently during the 19th century and the fishermen largely worked elsewhere, including the other Fisheries Society settlement of Pulteneytown, Caithness. In the second half of the 20th century larger craft, the east of Scotland fishermen and foreign boats with their attendant factory ships ('Klondykers') have again made Ullapool an active fishing port. It is the mainland terminal for the Stornoway car ferry and a busy tourist centre.

Shore Street (*above*)
Fronting the beach with panoramic views up **Loch Broom**, many houses are of *c*.1800 date, most altered, mostly with modern shopfronts. **Ornsay House**, *c*.1829 (former Church of Scotland manse paid for by the British Fisheries Society to house the minister for the 'Parliamentary' Church (see Argyll Street)) is a simple two-storey house with later additions and liberal use of contrasting paintwork.

56 **Caledonian MacBrayne** and the **Tourist Information Office** share a handsome harled warehouse, *c*.1790, three storeys high, truncated in late 1970s for road widening. It is matched by the similar **Captain's Cabin** on the corner of **Quay Street** opposite, which retains a forestair leading to its first-floor

'Captain's Cabin', a former storehouse, and Quay Street

doorway. Besides fishing gear, these warehouses may have been used to store salt for curing herring. A handsome cast-iron **memorial clock** stands in Quay Street, erected in 1889 to the memory of Sir John Fowler of Braemore and his family.

Above Fowler memorial clock. *Right* 'Parliamentary' Church

57 **Church of Scotland**, **Argyle Street**, 1829, Thomas Telford
Another 'Parliamentary' T-plan church, outer entrances flanking two central windows, all with depressed arched lintels. Windows retain original cast-iron lattice glazing. The five-sided gallery and 1829 fittings are rare survivals, indicative of the quality of the building in that it has deteriorated so little, despite having been out of use since 1929. The church was built to serve the expanding population of Ullapool for whom the parish church at Clachan, at the head of Loch Broom, was too distant (see p.89). During the summer months the church serves as a local museum.

Old Bank House, Argyle Street, early 19th century
Probably the first bank in Ullapool, its importance emphasised by its symmetrical frontage and slender columned portico.

Old Bank House

58 **Church of Scotland**, **Mill Street**, 1844, probably William Henderson
Former Free Church, a gaunt building not improved by later alterations. The two-storey red stone contemporary **manse** has a narrow recessed central bay. The small burial ground
59 at the corner of **Mill Street** and **Shore Street** may mark the site of a small chapel and graveyard in use before the 1829 church was built in Argyle Street.

Beaton

COIGACH, ISLE MARTIN & TANERA MORE

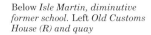

Strathkanaird and Coigach

The **Coigach** peninsula extends westwards, consisting mainly of crofting settlements (many cottages are now holiday homes). A 19th-century corn mill stands by the beach near **Achiltibuie** and a **salmon fishing station** at **Badentarbat**, its vaulted icehouse (1873) converted as a store and workroom. In **Isle Martin**, a fishing station with a customs house (for storage of taxable salt) was established in 1775 by a 'company of Liverpool gentlemen'. The customs house is still there, a simple two-storey dwelling-house doubled in size during the 20th century. The island has seen various vicissitudes – including the establishment of a flour-milling business in the 1930s (the grain brought in by sea – the venture did not prosper) and now a bird sanctuary. It boasts one of the smallest schools in the Highlands, measuring approximately 15 ft x 9 ft, constructed of corrugated-iron and lined throughout with boarded panelling. There are no longer any children to keep even this diminutive building in business.

60

Below Isle Martin, diminutive former school. Left Old Customs House (R) and quay

Historic Scotland

Historic Scotland

INVERLAEL & STRATH MORE

Tanera More, old herring station and pier

Historic Scotland

In the Parish Church at Clachan there is a mural memorial to Sir John Fowler (1817-88), Engineer-in-Chief to the Forth Railway Bridge, who lived at Braemore. His house has been demolished, but the gabled **stable range** stands close to the road. He owned land in **Strath More**, improved the farms, laid out the present field system, planted the gorge and, *c*.1870, constructed three 'very light bridges' over the **River Broom**. One of these is the handsome **Auchindrean Bridge**, *c*.1870, a rare lenticular (convex) truss of wrought-iron construction, the wooden deck suspended from the truss by lattice girders and linked to round masonry piers. Another is the **suspension foot-bridge** spanning the **Corrieshalloch Gorge** (National Trust for Scotland).

Tanera More, the largest of the **Summer Isles**, houses a large herring station with walled courtyard, established by 'Mr Roderick Morrison from Stornoway' in 1785. The long two-storey building was the home of the pioneer ecologist, Dr, later Sir, Frank Fraser-Darling in 1938, when he farmed on Tanera More and re-built the quay protecting the little harbour. As at Isle Martin, salmon cages moored in the bay indicate the fishing enterprises of the 1990s.

INVERLAEL & STRATH MORE
Inverlael Farm, *c*.1750
Symmetrical, white-harled house with a five-window frontage, probably the former spinning school and weaving manufactory established by the Trustees of the Annexed Estates in the mid-18th century in an attempt to introduce skills and industry to the Highlands. There were two other similar establishments, at **New Kelso**, **Lochcarron** (see p.103) and **Invermoriston** on Loch Ness. **Inverlael Bridge**, *c*.1790, was constructed as part of road improvements to Ullapool.

Below *Inverlael Farmhouse.*
Right *Auchindrean Bridge*

Beaton

Beaton

Hume

Left Lochbroom Parish church, Clachan. Above Simple galleried interior and unusual survival of pair parallel communion tables in centre

Lochbroom Parish Church, Clachan, 1817; bellcote 1878 by Matthews & Lawrie

An austere building in Strath More, a fertile valley confined by high hills at the head of Loch Broom. Plain square-headed windows are matched by smaller gallery lights.

'Purposefully simple interior', galleried on three sides with a rare double row of long communion tables down the centre fronting the demi-octagonal pulpit. There was a medieval chapel here when it was called Ballone, owned, as was Ballone Castle in Easter Ross, (see p.72) by the ubiquitous Mackenzies. In the burial ground there are 18th-century memorials to Mackenzies of Ballone and Dundonnell. **Glenview**, 1811, the old manse, is U-plan with extensive additions.

DUNDONNELL

Dundonnell House, 1767

Tall white-harled house with narrow windows punctuating its regular five-bay frontage, probably heightened c.1816; later dormers. The gardens are enclosed within early 19th-century rubble walls, adorned with an unusual early 20th-century glasshouse with curved

Lochbroom Parish Church was built in the year 1817. In 1831 a panic seized the congregation *causing a rush to be made to the doors and windows, by which many were crushed and bruised, though none killed. The alarm was given, not from any defect in the church, but the scream of a person seized with epilepsy; yet such was the effect of the shock on the nerves of the people that many of them could not be prevailed upon to enter the church again, unless it should undergo repair.*
New Statistical Account (1835)

Being left a free estate *worth £1600 a year, and some thousand pounds in money, he* [Kenneth Mackenzie of Dundonnell] *came home, settled on his property, completely changed the whole system of management which had been previously followed, introduced a superior breed of cattle for which he had a fine taste; bought valuable horses, with corresponding implements of husbandry and harness; greatly enlarged and improved his mansion house, built a fine square of offices, enclosed a large piece of ground for a garden, with a wall of stone and lime, ten or twelve feet high, which he laid out in the most tasteful manner, and stocked with a rich variety of fruit trees and bushes, as well as flowering shrubs and flowers; recovered an acre of waste land; opened up the country by new roads; built hundreds of yards of stone dykes; planted millions of firs and hard-wood trees; and in every way beautified and adorned his romantic little strath.*
New Statistical Account (1835)

Dundonnell House

Above *Woods and shelter belts planted by Kenneth Mackenzie of Dundonnell before 1832.*
Right *Dundonnell Bridge*

angles, and a Gothic Revival garden **ballroom** of *c*.1960 designed by Neil Roger. An 18th-century humpback bridge spans the Dundonnell River at the approach to the estate, enclosed in an idyllic wooded glen. The Mackenzies of Dundonnell settled here *c*.1700, and the original house may be incorporated in the mansion. The bosky, fertile nature of this beautiful, sheltered vale at the head of Little Loch Broom is due to the improving laird Kenneth Mackenzie (1801-32), who poured so much into the estate during his short life that it was sold after his death to pay his debts.

Scoraig
A crofting community re-established in the late 1960s/early 1970s on the north shores of Little Loch Broom, reached only by foot or by boat. About eighty people live at Scoraig, the new-style crofters drawn from many places and many walks of life. Old cottages have been renovated, primary and secondary schools established, new houses built. Electricity is generated by small windmills. One of the most remarkable of the new houses is **The Dome**, a low circular single-storey dwelling with a two-storey wing which is also round; both sections have conical roofs, the single storey covered with a turf thatch. The house was designed and built for his own use, *c*.1975, by Topher Dawson, boatbuilder.

The Dome

THE GAIRLOCH
Bounded by Gruinard Bay to the north the Gairloch embraces two sea lochs, **Loch Ewe** and **Loch Gairloch**, both enclosed by substantial headlands and bounded to landward by a mountainous hinterland, the coasts of which are a mosaic of small houses

and crofts. These settlements fringing the shore include **Laide**, **Aultbea**, **Mellon Udrigle**, **Mellon Charles**, **Midtown**, **Big Sand**, **Badachro** and **Port Henderson**. **Poolewe** and **Gairloch** (which has many named subdivisions) are the larger centres.

Gruinard House, a shooting lodge of many builds and little architectural distinction, stands by the shore overlooking the bay and Gruinard Island. The early 20th-century **estate cottages** with rounded dormer gables echo the style of Sir Robert Lorimer's Colinton cottages in Edinburgh. The simple, square and roofless medieval church of **Laide**, surrounded by a **burial ground**, lies close to the shore on the west side of Gruinard Bay.

Gruinard House estate cottages

1 **Udrigle House**, 1745
Amongst the most notable, even the most distinctive, surviving small lairds' houses in the Highlands, sited on the shores of Gruinard Bay. This plain, crowstepped two-storey house has a three-window façade, the slightly dropped central windows at different height to the outer. The north elevation is symmetrical with a centre doorway sheltered by a crowstepped 1756 porch. Notable interior fittings: very unusual ogee-shaped panelling, lugged doorcases and chimney-pieces and silhouette balusters on the staircase. The latter is built against the front wall of the house, lit by windows at half-landing stage (accounting for the irregular height of front centre windows; see also Applecross, p.101). The marriage stone in the parlour is inscribed 'W MK 1745 I MK' for one of the three William Mackenzies of the large and immensely complex family of Mackenzie of Gruinard.

Below Udrigle House, south front; the centre windows light stairwell. Bottom *Udrigle House and Gruinard Bay*

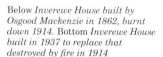

Top Aultbea. *Above* 'Clapper bridge', *the arches supported by stone slabs*

Aultbea, on the western side of Loch Ewe, straggles along the roadside encircling a small bay. **Free Church**, 1871-5, gaunt Gothic flanked by a nondescript 1980s **manse** (replacing a large late 19th-century gabled house). The **seven-span clapper bridge**, probably mid 19th-century, has been bypassed and restored. These simple structures, with rubble piers spanned by single stone slabs, were easier to build than arched bridges and in the Highlands are found in both Wester Ross and NW Sutherland.

POOLEWE

Below Inverewe House *built by* Osgood Mackenzie *in 1862, burnt down 1914. Bottom* Inverewe House *built in 1937 to replace that destroyed by fire in 1914*

At the head of a small bay opening from Loch Ewe, Poolewe is best known as the nearest 62 village to **Inverewe Gardens**, established by Osgood Mackenzie after 1862. However, Poolewe was the site of the Red Smiddy, the earliest iron blast furnace in Scotland, in operation from between 1610 to 1670, which exploited the local natural woodland (now only evident on the islands in Loch Maree). Other furnace sites were at Fasagh and Furnace (close to Letterewe) on the north side of Loch Maree, and Talladale and Slattadale on the south shores of the same loch.

Inverewe House, 1937,
Tarbolton and Ochterlony
Simple white-harled house, with sweeping roof
and long 1930s horizontal windows
overlooking the bay, built by Mrs Mairi
Sawyer to replace the 1862 baronial home
constructed by her father, Osgood Mackenzie,
destroyed by fire in 1914. Internationally
celebrated sub-tropical gardens in which palm
trees can frame a view of the Hebrides; of
outstanding beauty and horticultural interest.
The National Trust for Scotland, which has
owned Inverewe since 1952, built a **Visitors'
Centre** at the entrance designed by W
Schomberg Scott, 1965, extended in 1979 by
Ian Begg. This long, low white building
welcomes and accommodates a stream of
visitors to the famous gardens, into which it
blends in a kindly fashion. New competition-
winning restaurant exploiting existing garden
woods and coastal panorama by Richard
Murphy and Graeme Montgomery, under
development. *Gardens only, open daily;
guidebook available*

Inverewe, NTS reception centre

Shrondubh, 1730-40, possibly with earlier
core, is a regularly fronted two-storey white
house with two barns, one long and low
flanking the road. Tall **Cliff House**, *c.*1800,
overlooks the bay. **Poolewe Church**, 1828,
Thomas Telford, is of standard 'Parliamentary'
pattern. The **Old Manse**, also 1828, Thomas
Telford, was originally single-storey standard
H-plan, sympathetically heightened to two
storeys.

Below *Shrondubh.*
Middle *Poolewe Church.*
Bottom *Former Nurses' Home*

Former Nurses' Home, 1912,
A Maitland & Sons
Pleasant design with shaped hood-moulds and
panelled pilastered entrance, generous
windows and pretty, original decorative frosted
glazing to inner main door. The 'surgery', with
its separate side entrance, is now the local
District Council office. An inscribed plaque
records that this building was erected *In
memory of Mary, Lady Mackenzie, with money
left for that purpose by Dr Charles Robertson
late of Achtercairn, Gairloch.* Lady Mary was
the widowed mother to Osgood Mackenzie,
who devoted much of his life to improving the

Top *Bank Barn; byre in ground floor with storage over.* Middle *Bank Barn with access to upper floor from slope.* Above *Carn Dearg Youth Hostel*

Above *Strath.* Right *27 Big Sand, a traditional thatched cottage lived in until June 1981*

lot of the crofters on the family estate; the Nurses' Home is a unique witness of medical philanthropy in the Highlands.

Close to the church lies one of the very few **bank barns** north of Mallaig and the Lochaber coast: a simple rectangular 19th-century building constructed to exploit the slope with byre and stable accommodation in the lower floor and access to first-floor loft from the hillside above.

Strath

Neat 19th-century two-storey houses line the village street, more cottages spilling out over the hillside. **Strathgair House**, 1805, a former manse, is the usual substantial two-storey house with projecting drawing- and dining-room wing added in 1823. Later 19th-century **Carn Dearg** (Youth Hostel), a gabled villa whose tall square chimney stacks punctuate the skyline, stands silhouetted on the cliff edge overlooking Gairloch Bay, an encouraging landmark for many weary hostellers.

27 Big Sand, 19th century

Traditional croft cottage with thatched roof and thatched chimney stack. These 'hinging lums' were originally a standard fitting in cottages, the internal wooden or wattle hearth canopy tapering into a flue and rounded wooden-framed chimney, thatched and well daubed with clay or mud to prevent fire. Instead of thatched lums, sometimes plain square wooden stacks capped the flue; clay drain-pipes and even a bottomless metal

bucket served the purpose! As peat was the principal fuel, there were few sparks and the apparently combustible material was reasonably fireproof. Once the standard dwelling, these little rubble cottages with their tiny windows and thatched roofs are a rarity. Hopefully, steps will be taken to conserve this now scarce example. It is encouraging that the only other traditional thatched cottage in the Gairloch, **11 Melvaig**, sited in a coastal township further north from Big Sand, was restored and re-thatched in 1990.

Thatched cottages in the Gairloch,
Top 27 Big Sand Above 11 Melvaig

Gairloch Museum, housed in a
disused farm steading; re-sited
Rubha Reidh Lighthouse lantern at
left

Gairloch Museum

A converted 19th-century steading, the byre making a most attractive restaurant, where some record of local crofting, fishing and other aspects of Gairloch traditional life is to be found. The domed light and glass prism from **Rubha Reidh Lighthouse**, 1912, D A Stevenson, were donated to the museum after automation in 1988 and sympathetically incorporated into the building. *Open during summer season; local literature available*

Gairloch Hotel, 1872 and 1880,
A Maitland & Sons

Tall gabled range with canted outer bays: earlier house at rear. Tourism, no novelty to Gairloch, required this imposing hotel for visitors and travellers well over a century ago. The **Free Church**, 1878, by Matthews & Lawrie, is large and Gothic on a prominent site. Its **manse**, *c*.1844, a plain house with regular three-window frontage. The **burial ground** is a medieval chapel site and contains fragments of an earlier church, replaced across the road by a small, plain **kirk** in 1781, recast 1908 by A Maitland & Sons.

Gairloch Bay with Free Church of
Scotland; Gairloch Hotel (R)

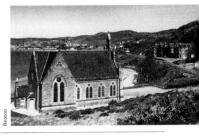

FLOWERDALE

Bank of Scotland

Bank of Scotland, *c.*1985, Tom Alexander, Bank of Scotland architects
Unusual Swiss chalet-style timber banking hall on deep rubble base. The 19th-century adjoining dormered premises are a marked contrast.

Craeg Hastin, designed for himself by Kenneth Gunn, a local electrician, in 1946, using many books. 30s style with innovatory electrical provision.

The 18th-century M-gable of Flowerdale House (*above*) is peculiar to Wester Ross and West Sutherland, the earliest example being the ruinous Calda or Eddercalda House on the shores of Loch Assynt, 1727. Its plan was inspired probably by the military designers of similarly gabled Bernera and Ruthven Barracks a year or two earlier. The result is a much deeper house than normal with generous internal space.

64 **Flowerdale House,** 1738 (*above and left*)
Fine laird's house whose regular front has a central gable, and long round-headed windows lighting the principal first-floor rooms. The main entrance, with moulded and corniced doorway, is approached up a flight of stairs. The building is M-gabled and two rooms deep, the gables crowstepped and capped by corniced, string-coursed chimney stacks. Low swept dormers light the attics. The 1904 addition by A Maitland & Sons extends continuously at west, doubling the size of the house but designed in sympathetic scale with the original dwelling – similar swept dormers, crowsteps and projecting bowed bay. The house was built by Alexander Mackenzie of Gairloch and his wife (and cousin) Janet Mackenzie of Scatwell (see p.46) whose initials, together with the date, are inscribed on the east gable skew-puts. The property is still owned by the Mackenzies of Gairloch and Conon, Easter Ross (see p.41).

Left *Flowerdale Barn. The round-headed doorways at each end are later insertions.* Above *Coat of Arms of Alexander and Janet Mackenzie of Gairloch*

Flowerdale Barn, 1730

Perhaps the earliest *dated* barn in Scotland. A fine long rubble building with regular tooled-margined rectangular openings venting the loft which is reached by a gable forestair. Also constructed by Alexander and Janet Mackenzie, who were married in that year, their fine coat of arms over the centre winnowing door and initials and date on the loft door lintel.

Kerry Falls Power Station, 1951, W Taylor

Rectangular with long windows, walls of local red stone with similar margins to all openings, and a piended roof of Caithness slates. Scottish Hydro-Electric have displayed commendable sympathy in choice of material and design to suit the site. **Kerrysdale**, a plain house of *c*.1800, has a long cruck-framed barn at the rear.

Aird House, Badachro, *c*.1840 is fronted by jetties which served fishing boats in this sheltered bay. There is an unusually complete

The Tigh Dige or *Moat House was so called because the original house belonging to us, which was down in the hollow between the present mansion, was surrounded by a moat and drawbridge. The first Sir Alexander ... started building the present house in 1738, and as it was the very first instance in all the country round of a slated house, the old name Tigh Dige was continued, with the addition given to it of **nam gorm Leac** (of the blue slabs) ... some English tourists, finding the lovely Baile Mor Glen peculiarly rich in wild flowers, proposed to my ancestor that it should be named Flowerdale. I am thankful to say I have never in the course of my long life heard the house called otherwise in Gaelic than (An) Tigh Dige and the place **am Baile Mor** (The Great Town or home).*
Osgood Mackenzie, *A Hundred Years in the Highlands* (1921)

Left *Kerrysdale; interior of cruck framed barn. The cruck blades, originally linked at their apex to form a series of arches supporting the heavy thatched roof, have been shortened to accommodate the shallower pitch of the later corrugated-iron roof.* Above *Kerry Falls Power Station*

The twenty miles' drive (from Achnasheen), *through a desolate, wild and perfectly uninhabited country, was beautiful... from the top of the hill you go down a very grand pass called Glen Dochart. Here Loch Maree came in view most beautifully.*
Queen Victoria Sept. 1877

fishing station on **Eilean Tioram** opposite. At **South Erradale** a mid 19th-century 14-arched rubble **viaduct** carries the road to Redpoint over marshy ground.

Letterewe House,
from late 18th century onwards
Many additions have transformed Letterewe, standing on a green pocket of land fronting **Loch Maree**, into a white-harled baronial shooting lodge. The pretty, little **watch-house** by the jetty has an oriel window with a glazed niche to house a light to guide boats across the loch, for Letterewe can be reached only by boat – or by many miles of footpath. There are two long cruck-framed **barns** (one is now converted as a cottage) besides other outbuildings and formerly a small school. Letterewe, originally a Mackenzie laird's house, was a *'good seat'* in 1813.

Loch Maree Hotel, garden front

66 **Loch Maree Hotel**, 1872, A Maitland & Sons Gabled, red sandstone frontage aggrandised by a gilded Royal coat of arms but spoilt by fire-escapes and flat-roofed extensions. The rear of the building, overlooking Loch Maree, remains the *'nice little house'* where Queen Victoria spent a few days in September 1877. She travelled from Balmoral by train, completing the final twenty miles from Achnasheen in a horse-drawn 'sociable', the staff following in a wagonette and traps. A long inscription in Gaelic on a boulder in front of the hotel records the event.

TORRIDON

Loch Torridon Hotel (formerly Ben-damph Lodge)

67 **Coulin Lodge**, 1869
Plain and gabled red sandstone shooting lodge with contrasting pale dressings, built for Lord Elphinstone who had bought the estate three years earlier. It provided accommodation for shooting party guests and accompanying servants. The chapel for family prayers is lit by pointed-headed Gothic windows giving a suitable ecclesiastical touch. The baronial **Loch Torridon Hotel**, formerly Ben-damph Lodge, 1884-7, by Alexander Ross, stands on the shores of Loch Torridon. The clock tower, housing entrance porch in base, is inscribed JUBILAE VICTORIAE 1887.

Torridon Youth Hostel set against the high tops of Liathach

Torridon Youth Hostel, 1975,
Moira & Moira
Award-winning development hunched low into the hillside against the weather: a cluster of harled cottage-like blocks. From a distance they form a series of white specks dwarfed by the majestic bulk of Liathach. Spacious blockwork dining hall open to the rafters within.

The crofting townships of **Inveralligin** and **Alligin Shuas** hug the coast below towering **Beinn Alligin**, the road continuing as far as **Lower Diabeg**. Here the neat rubble pier, 1902, C R Manners, exploits the harbourage afforded by Loch Diabeg.

Shieldaig is a linear village of 19th-century and later houses strung out along the shore. Single-storey former manse, 1825, Thomas Telford; his 'Parliamentary' church (see pp.4-5) was destroyed by fire and replaced by the present plain edifice. Shieldaig is in the Parish of Applecross, the Parish Church far from Shieldaig and accessible only by boat or footpath until the road arrived in 1976.

'An Aird' corrugated-iron cottage: 'crinkly tin' enjoyed a vogue in the Highlands as elsewhere

Below *'Old Inn', typical one-and-a half storey house.* Left *Shieldaig*

APPLECROSS

Linear settlement at Lonbain

Below Fine panelled pulpit with *sounding board. Bottom* Applecross church

APPLECROSS

The name has nothing to do with holy fruit but is derived from *Apor* (Gaelic for Aber) = mouth and *Crossan* = stream, the confluence of the river that flows through the wide sheltered Strath to the inner sound. The River Applecross is known locally as the Crossan and the parish as Comeraich, Gaelic for sanctuary. The Applecross peninsula was accessible only by sea, footpath or the steep road from the south over the Bealach na Ba until the north road was opened in 1976. This hugs the coastline, linking Shieldaig with Applecross, via the townships of **Kenmore**, **Fearnbeg** and **Fearnmore**, passing close to the deserted linear settlement of **Lonbain**. That a house of the size and quality of Applecross House, together with church, manse and village, should be built where it is, on a fertile coastal strip cut off by mountainous terrain, demonstrates the importance of sea transport in the past. Isolation is only recent, sea communication having formerly linked Applecross with important local centres on the mainland and in the Western Isles.

Applecross Church, 1817

Simple rectangular church lit by four long windows, a doorway in each outer bay. The inside is somewhat over-restored, the walls stripped back to the local red rubble. The handsome panelled double-decker pulpit has been moved from its original site in the centre of the south wall while the Celtic cross housed in the church once stood in the burial ground. This was the site of a monastery founded in AD 673 by St Maelrubha. Note cast-iron tombstone of 1832 in burial ground – almost certainly brought to Applecross by sea from iron-works in the south of Scotland. The **Old Manse**, 1796, close to the church, is a tall, white-harled, three-storey house with small single-storey flanking wings.

Applecross House, c.1730-40
Tall, three-storey house with attics and low single-storey wings projecting to form east courtyard. Crowstepped and M-gabled (as Flowerdale, p.96), the main entrance is through the regular rear courtyard. The five-window front has similarities with Udrigle (see p.91): dropped centre windows light the half-landings of the staircase built against the front wall, the lower made into a doorway in 19th century, leading from a glazed porch of the same date. Re-used date-stone of 1675.

Applecross House; 'M' gable like Flowerdale. The porch is later, the original entrance at the rear. Lower centre window lights staircase set against front wall

RCAHMS

Applecross Mains, a mid-19th-century farm square, is flanked by the **Crac Barn** of the same period. This large stone barn has wattled and louvred openings. Pair of earlier stores known as **Top Barns** are sited on an exposed knoll, aligned to direct the prevailing west winds to dry stored hay and unthreshed corn. These long, low, rectangular barns have rubble walls and wide staved vents; originally both were heather thatched, one now roofed with corrugated-iron. They were said to be more effective as ventilated stores than the more sophisticated, but sheltered, **Crac Barn** in the hollow by the Mains.

RCAHMS

Applecross Mains, heather thatched 'Top Barn', one of a pair of low, ventilated barns

Milton, the village centre, probably replaces a settlement clustered around Applecross House. It consists principally of a long row of cottages facing the sea. The one dated 1867, with a salmon carved on the date-stone, indicates commercial salmon netting.

The present **parish church** is at **Camusterrach** (former 1845 Free Church) with plain attendant **manse** of same period; there is a scatter of cottages here at **Ard-dubh** and **Toscaig** – all simple buildings, fo*r 'every man is architect of his own house'.*

KISHORN, LOCHCARRON & GLEN CARRON

Courthill House, **Kishorn**, 19th century
Tall gabled, roofless mansion. The rear service quarters are intact, and through the courtyard arch is the small **Episcopal Chapel** built by Lady Murray of Courthill in 1901, her architect Alexander Ross. Plain interior with Romanesque chancel; bust of unknown lady, 1848, H Weeks, sculptor. The chapel is still in occasional use.

Top Milton village. Middle above Ard-dhubh. Middle Courthill House, sketched before demolition. Above Tiny estate cottage, Courthill. Right Kishorn, Courthill Episcopal Chapel

Old Lochcarron Parish Church

Lochcarron (originally Janetown) consisted of only a few houses until 1813, when it tripled in size after being reached by the 'Parliamentary' road from Contin to Strome through Glen Carron. The old **burial ground** marks the medieval chapel site; the ruins are those of the church built in 1751 and abandoned when re-placed in turn by the **Old Church** at Kirkton, *c.*1840. This stands a little way eastwards of the village, its white-harled bulk with four tall pointed-headed windows conspicuous as a landmark when viewed from the south side of Loch Carron.

Houses date mainly from 19th century though the gabled **Lochcarron Hotel** is a little earlier. **Free Church**, 1846, alterations, 1859, Ross & Joass, has round-arched windows with intersecting glazing bars. There is a **Church of Scotland** of *c*.1900. Little remains of 15th-century **Strome Castle**, blown up by Kenneth Mackenzie of Kintail in 1602. There is no longer a ferry over the sea loch to the village of Strome Ferry (District of Skye & Lochalsh).

Lochcarron Free Church of Scotland

68 **Tullich Farm**, 18th century onwards
Farmhouse and farm buildings laid out in U-plan: simple farmhouse flanked by later wings. The open-sided rubble barn, approximately 120 ft long, is one of the longest of this type (see p.6). It has two pairs of opposing winnowing doors, rather than one, flanked by large louvred and wattled vents. The cruck blades have been sawn off, and the heavy heather-thatched roof they supported replaced by corrugated iron.

69 **New Kelso**, *c*.1753
Long two-storey linen spinning and weaving school and factory, one of those established in the Highlands by the Trustees of the Annexed Estates (the others at **Inverlael**, Lochbroom (p.88) and **Invermoriston** (Loch Ness). Ninian Jeffrey from Kelso was the first manager of the New Kelso School – hence the Borders name. The **farm square** has cruck-framed louvred **barn** and **byre** constructed in the local vernacular tradition.

Similar construction to the Tullich Barn was used locally for domestic housing in the 17th and 18th century. The Revd Aeneas Sage, Minister of Lochcarron, brought his bride in 1728 to *the manse* (which) *was constructed after the fashion of all Highland houses about the end of the seventeenth century. About 100 feet long, the walls were built of stone for about three feet in height about the foundation, and around the roots of the couples* (cruck trusses), *which were previously fixed in the ground; over this were several layers of turf or fail, so as to bring the wall to the height of 10 feet. About half the house was taken up by three rooms and a kitchen, the remainder contained the cow byre.*
Donald Sage, *Memorabilia Domestica* (1899)

New Kelso - former 18th-century linen 'manufactory'

Top *Loch Carron.*
Above *Achnashellach Lodge*

The Stage to Strome Ferry (for Kyle) *is very hilly and few of the hills have much to recommend them. But it was a beautiful drive, because much of it lay along Loch Alshe and Loch Carron.* Lord Cockburn, *Circuit Journeys* (1841)

Strathcarron Railway Station, 1870, was opened by the Dingwall & Skye Railway which went as far as Strome Ferry, but was extended to Kyle of Lochalsh in 1897. **Atterdale House**, dated 1755, has an earlier (or old-fashioned) corniced doorpiece and 19th-century additions. **Achnashellach Lodge**, *c.*1870 but probably incorporating earlier building, is gabled and grandiose: the room above the deep projecting porch is an unusual feature in a Highland shooting lodge. The lodge stands beside the A890 linking **Glen Carron** with the A832, **Garve** and **Dingwall**.

Right *Sturdy, naive tombstone standing in Old Lochcarron burial ground. It was 'ERECTED by John MacDonald to the memory of his Father William MacDonald late tenant Coulags Who departed this life on the 24th June 1838 Aged 90'. Coulags is a farm in Glen Carron*

ACKNOWLEDGEMENTS AND BIBLIOGRAPHY

The author is particularly grateful to David Alston, Laurie Beaton, John Duncan, Anne Riches, David Walker, Geoffrey Stell and Andrew Wright for their continued help, advice and encouragement during the preparation of this Guide. Thanks are due to all who have enabled her to visit and photograph their properties.

Assistance has also been given by : Catherine Cruft, Ian Gow, Simon Green, Shona MacGaw, Ruth Wimberley and Leslie Ferguson, National Monuments Record; Pam Craig, John Hume and Deborah Mays, Historic Scotland; Dan Ross, Scottish Hydro-Electric plc; John Baldwin; Malcolm Bangor-Jones; Manager, Balblair Distillery; Ian Begg; Monica Clough; Jane Durham; David Somerville; Brian Stewart and Graham Watson, Ross & Cromarty District Council; T W Fraser, Bank of Scotland; Topher Dawson; Janis Dawson; M L Dunley, British Alcan Highland Smelters Ltd; John Gifford; Rosemary Mackenzie, Tain Museum; Elizabeth Marshall; Les Hunter, Douglas T Forrest, Architects; Graham Wilson, Elgin Library; M G O'Brien, Highland Region Library Service; The Rector, Fortrose Academy; Margaret Richardson; Margaret Smith together with the Avoch Heritage Society.

Graham Douglas, John Hume and Elizabeth Whitfeld have kindly and skillfully executed drawings. Other illustrations would not have been possible without assistance from the following individuals or organisations: Joanna Close-Brooks; Drummond & Co, WS, Edinburgh (papers of D and J S Campbell, WS, SRO RHP12645, with approval of the Keeper, SRO); Dundee Art Gallery & Museums; Highland Maps, Alness; Historic Scotland (Crown Copyright); M I Leslie Melville; National Trust for Scotland; Royal Commission on the Ancient & Historical Monuments of Scotland (Crown Copyright); Jytte Piggott; Douglas Scott, Elgin Photo Centre; Scottish Record Office; Captain R Stirling; Tain & District Museum; Andrew Thoms; Bruce Urquhart; Messrs J & W Wittet, Elgin. As is usual in the series the illustration source is credited beside each one.

The Firthlands of Ross and Sutherland (ed.) John Baldwin, 1986; **Studies in Scottish Antiquity** (ed.) David Breeze, 1984; **Exploring Scotland's Heritage, The Highlands**, Joanna Close-Brooks, 1986; **Two Houses**, Monica Clough, 1990; **Biographical Dictionary of British Architects 1600-1840**, Howard Colvin, 1978; **Gairloch**, J H Dixon, 1886; **Victorian Architects**, F Dixon and S Muthesius, 1978; **The British Fisheries Society 1786-1893**, Jean Dunlop, 1978; **Annals of the Free Church ii** (ed.) W Ewing, 1914; **Shetland: An Illustrated Architectural Guide**, Mike Finnie, 1990; **Island Farm**, Frank Fraser-Darling, 1943; **Architects in the Highlands in the 19th century: A Sketch**, Bulletin 7, Scottish Georgian Society (AHSS), John Gifford, 1980; **Ordnance Gazetteer of Scotland**, Francis H Groome, 1882-5; **New Ways through the Glens**, A R B Haldane, 1962; **Monarchs of the Glen**, Duff Hart-Davis, 1978; **The Architecture of Scottish Post-Reformation Churches 1560-1843**, George Hay, 1957; **The Industrial Archaeology of Scotland ii**, John R Hume, 1977; **Imperial Gazetteer of Scotland**, *c.*1855; **Kinkell: The Reconstruction of a Scottish Castle**, Gerald Laing, 1974; **Encyclopaedia of Cottage, Farm and Villa Architecture**, J C Loudon, 1846; **Castellated and Domestic Architecture of Scotland**, David MacGibbon and Thomas Ross, 1887-92; **The Ecclesiastical Architecture of Scotland**, David MacGibbon and Thomas Ross, 1896-7; **Old Ross-shire and Scotland**, W MacGill, 1909-11; **Telford's Highland Churches**, Allan Maclean, 1989; **A Hundred Years in the Highlands**, Osgood Mackenzie, 1921; **A General Review of the Agriculture of the Counties of Ross and Cromarty**, Sir George Steuart Mackenzie, 1813; **William Forsyth, Esq**, Hugh Miller, 1839; **Easter Ross 1750-1850: The Double Frontier**, Ian R M Mowat, 1981; **Tain through the Centuries**, R W & Jean Munro, 1966; **Scottish Lighthouses**, R W Munro, 1979; **Highland Bridges**, Gillian Nelson, 1990; **New Statistical Account**, 1845; **The Ross and Cromarty Book** (ed.) Donald Omand, 1984; **Picts**, Anna Ritchie, 1983; **Statutory List of Buildings of Special Architectural or Historic Interest, Ross & Cromarty District**, SDD, 1983; **Edwardian Architecture**, Alastair Service, 1977; **The Statistical Account of Scotland**, (ed.) Sir John Sinclair, 1791-9; **The Military Roads in Scotland**, William Taylor, 1976; **Discovering the Black Isle**, Douglas Willis, 1989. Also various local guidebooks.

INDEX

A

Achiltibuie 87
Achnashellach Lodge,
  Glen Carron 104
Adam, Robert 56
Aird House, Badachro 97
Aitken, David 44
Aldie Mill, Tain 81
Alexander, Tom 96
Allangrange House 13
Allangrange, Old 13
Alness 59-61
  Academy 61
  Dalmore House 61
  Masonic Hall 60
  Perrins Centre 60
  Teaninich House 60-1
Angus, George 79
Ankerville, Nigg 70
Applecross 4, 100-2
  House 101
  Mains 101
  Milton 102
Arabella, Invergordon 68
Ardross Castle 62
Ardullie Lodge, Kiltearn 57
Arts & Crafts style 13-14, 21
Assynt House, Glen Glass 58
Atterdale House,
  Strathcarron 104
Auchindrean Bridge 88
Aultbea 92
Aultgowrie Gate Lodge 43
Avoch 15-16

B

Badentarbat 8, 87
Balblair Distillery 83
Balblair Inn 37
Balfour, Arthur 46
Ballone Castle 5, 72
Balnagown Castle 5, 65-6
bank barns 94
Baxter, John II 70
Bayfield House, Nigg 69-70
Begg, Ian 93
Beveridge, Laurence 79
Big Sand, Gairloch 94
Black Isle 6, 9-38
Blanc, Hippolyte J 76
Boag, James 37, 53
Boniface, St 17
Braelangwell, Resolis 36
Brahan Castle 44
Brahan Seer (Coinneach
  Odhar) 24
Brown, Thomas 30, 55, 77
Burgerhuys, Michael 76
Burn, George 55
Burn, William 10
Burnett, J Russell 49
Burnett, T S 79
Burnthouse, Avoch 15

C

Cadboll
  Castle 71
  Cliff House 71
Cadell, William A 43
cairns 4
Caisteal Corach 56

Carruthers, W L 13, 21
Castle Craig 38
Castle Leod 50
castles 5
Caulfield, Major 46
Chambers, Robert 47
Chanonry 23-4
  Lighthouse 23
  Point 23, 24
churches 4-5:
  Allangrange chapel 12
  Alness 59-60
  Applecross 100-1
  Ardgay (Sutherland) 82
  Ardross 62
  Arpafeelie Episcopal 12
  Aultbea Free Church 92
  Avoch 15, 16
  Bogallan Free Church 12
  Camusterrach 102
  Chapelhill 70
  Collegiate Church
    Tain 76
  Contin 44-5
  Cromarty Episcopal
    Church 30
  Cromarty Gaelic
    Church 32
  Cromarty Old Church 29
  Dingwall Free Church 53
  Edderton 81-2
  Fearn Abbey 70-1
  Fortrose Cathedral 4,
    18-19
  Fortrose Parish
    Church 22
  Invergordon 64
  Kilchrist Chapel 40
  Kilmuir 12
  Kilmuir Easter 67
  Kiltearn 58
  Kinlochluichart 46-7
  Kirkmichael 37
  Kishorn Episcopal
    Chapel 102
  Knockbain, Munlochy
    12
  Laide 91
  Lochbroom Parish
    Church 89
  Lochcarron 102-3
  Logie Easter 68
  Loth (Sutherland) 82
  Lower Gledfield 82
  Milton Free Church 46
  Nigg 68-9
  Old Logie & Urquhart
    Wester Church 38
  Poolewe 93
  Redcastle 11
  Resolis 37
  Rosemarkie 23
  Rosskeen, Invergordon 65
  St Andrew, Fortrose 20
  St Anne's Episcopal
    Church 50
  St Clement's, Dingwall 55
  St Duthac, Tain 77
  St James the Great,
    Dingwall 54
  St Peter & St Boniface,
    Fortrose 19-20
  St Vincent de Paul,
    Tain 77, 78

Strath Conon, Carnoch 46
Strathpeffer 49
Strathpeffer Free
  Church 49
Tain Collegiate Church 4
Tain Free Church 78
Tain Parish Church 77
Tarbat Free Church 74
Tarbat Old Parish
  Church 74
Ullapool 86
Urquhart & Ferintosh 38
Urray Parish Church 43-4
Clark, John 75
Cleveland Bridge
  Engineering Co 44
Coigach 87
Commission for Highland
  Roads & Bridges 3, 55,
  61
Comper, Sir Ninian 30
Conon Bridge 7, 41-2
Conon House 41
Contin 44-6
Contin Bridge 3, 45
Coul House 19, 45-6
Courthill House, Kishorn
  102
Cromarty 24-34
  Bellevue 31
  Big Vennel 34,
  Braehead 33
  Church Street 6, 9-32
  Courthouse 30
  fishertown 34
  Forsyth House 32
  Gordon's Lane 34
  Hemp Works or
    Ropeworks 33
  High Street 32
  House 25-6
  Hugh Miller's Cottage 31
  Mercat Cross 30
  Miller House 31
  Old Brewery 28
  Old Manse (Gardener's
    House) 27
  Tolbooth 30
  Townlands Barn 32
Cromarty Firth Viaduct
  10, 57
Crouch & Hogg 10, 44, 57
Crouch, Hogg, Waterman
  & Ove Arup 81
Cullicudden 37, 45

D

Dal-Neich Bridge 61
Dawson, Topher 90
Devey, Richard & Robert
  45
Dingwall 51-6
  Castle 54
  Castle Street 54
  Courthouse and Police
    Station 55
  Cromartie obelisk 54, 55
  High Street 52, 53-4
  Neil Gunn Road 56
  Tolbooth 6, 52, 53
Dingwall, Thomas 74
Disruption (1843) 5

Drynie Mains, Kilmuir 12
Dublin village 62
Dundonnell House 89-90
Duthus, St 75

E

East Lodge, Kildary 68
Easter Fearn bridge 61
Easter Ross 6, 39-83
Edderton 81-3
  Eastburn House 82
  Fearn Lodge 83
  Mains 83
  Mid Fearn 83
  Old Manse 82
  Wester Fearn 83
Eilean Tioram 98
Evanton 58-9

F

Fairburn Tower 5, 43
Fearn Abbey 4, 70-1
Fearn Railway Station 71
Ferryton Point girnal 37
Fisher, Admiral 'Jackie' 63
Flockhart, William 13, 14, 21
Flowerdale Barn, Gairloch 96
Flowerdale House,
  Gairloch 96
Fodderty 51
Forbes, Thomas 78
Forsyth, William 25, 32
Fortrose 17-22
  Academy 20-1
  Academy Street 20
  Cathedral 4, 18-19
  Deanery 20
  High Street 21-2
  Kindeace Lodge 21
  Platcock House 22
  Town Hall 22
  Town House 19
  forts 4
Foulis 56-7
Foulis Castle 6, 56-7
Foulis Ferry Renthouse
  57-8
Fraser-Darling, Sir Frank
  88
Free Church of Scotland 5
Fyrish Monument 59

G

Gairloch, The 90-8
  Bank of Scotland 96
  Craeg Hastin 96
  Hotel 95
  Museum 95
Garve 46
Geanies House 72
Gibb, Sir Alexander &
  Partners 47
girnals 6, 37
Glenmorangie 81
Gracie, A 71
Graham, James Gillespie
  23, 65, 68
Green, N E 43
Groome, Francis H 52
Gruinard House, Gairloch 91
Gunn, Kenneth 96

H

Hartfield, Tain 81
Henderson, William 86
High Mills, Tain 81
Hill of Fearn 71
'hinging lums' 94-5

I

Inver 71
Inverewe Gardens 92, 93
Inverewe House *92*, 93
Invergordon 63-8
  British Alcan
    Smelter 64
  Cromarty Firth Port
    Authority 64
  High Street 64
  Kincraig 64-5
  Kindeace House 64
  Mutiny *63*
  Newmore Castle 65
Inverlael Bridge 88
Inverlael Farm 88
Isle Martin 87

J

James IV, King *75*
James V, King *75*
Jemimaville 35
Joass, W C 49, 53, 55, 56

K

Kay, James Sandford 56
Kelton House, 68
Kennedy, G R M &
  Partners 22
Kerry Falls Power Station
  96
Kessock Bridge 3, *9*, 10
Kilcoy Castle 6, 11
Kildermorie 63
Kilmuir 12
Kiltearn 57-8
Kilvannie Manor Hotel 51
Kinkell 42
Kirkwood, M 21
Kishorn 102
Knockbreck House, Tain 81

L

Ladyhill (Ormond) 5
Laing, Gerald 42
Lawrie, William 24
Letterewe House 98
Lindsay, Ian 42
Linklater, Eric 70
Loch Maree Hotel 98
Lochbroom *89*
Lochcarron 102-3
Lonbain, Applecross *3*, 100
Lorimer, Sir Robert 56, 91
Loudon, J C 66
Lower Diabeg 99
Lutyens, Sir Edwin 14

M

Macdonald Memorial
  Tower 56

MacFarlane of Glasgow
  73
McHardy, John 33, 58
Mackenzies of Coul 19,
  45
Mackenzies of Rosehaugh
  13
Mackenzie, Sir George 13
Mackenzie, Sir George,
  1st Earl of Cromartie
  72, *73*
Mackenzie, Sir George
  Steuart *45*
Mackenzie, Hector 74
Mackenzie, William 54
Mackintosh, William 40
McQuirter, William 61
Maelrubha, St 4, 45, 100
Maitland, A. & Sons 60,
  61, 63, 64, 68, 69,
  74, 76, 77, 78, 79,
  93-6, 98
Maitland, Andrew 55, 56,
  75, *77*, 80
Manners, C R 99
Marybank, Strath Conon
  44
Marybank, Kildary 68
Matheson, Robert 76
Matthews & Lawrie 22,
  24, 89, 95
Meikle Daan, Edderton 83
Meikle Ferry viaduct 81
Melvaig, Gairloch 95
Millbuie 38
Miller, Hugh 31, *32*, *37*,
  41
Milton, Invergordon 67
Milton, Strathconon 44
Mitchell, Joseph 41, 71
Moira & Moira 99
Montgomery, Graeme 93
Mossford Power Station
  47
Mowat, Charles Loch *63*
Moy Bridge 44
Muir of Ord 39-40
  Highfield House estate
    40
  Ord Distillery 39
  Tarradale Mains 40
  Tomich House 39
Munlochy 12-14
Munro, Thomas 38
Murison, Thomas 15
Murphy, Richard 93
Murray, D A 64
Murray, Kenneth 79

N

New Kelso 103
Newhall, Resolis 36
Nigg 68-70
Novar House, Evanton 59

O

Ormond Castle 5, 12, 16

P

'Parliamentary' churches 5
Paye, The, Cromarty *2*, 32

Pearson, J L 54
Perrins, Charles William
  Dyson *62*
Pitcalzean, Nigg 70
Poolewe 92-3
  Cliff House 93
  District Council Office
    (Former Nurses'
    Home) 93
  Shrondubh 93
Portmahomack 73
Poyntzfield, Resolis 35-6

R

railway network 4
Redcastle *5*, 10-11
Reid, A & W 77
Resolis 35-8
Rhind, George 15
Rhind, John 12, 22, 53
Ritchie, Handyside 32
Robertson, John 20, 22,
  23, 50, 67
Robertson, William 39, 53,
  55, 77, 80
Rockfield Castle (Little
  Tarrel) 71
Roger, Neil 90
Rosehaugh House, Avoch
  13-14, 44
Rosemarkie 22-3
Roskill farmhouse 13
Ross & Joass 15, 42, 64, 103
Ross & Macbeth 11, 20,
  38, 42, 62, 77
Ross, Alexander 12, 15,
  16, 21, 45, 54, 60, 62,
  64, 65, 70, 77, 98, 102
Ross and Cromarty
  District 4
Ross, George *25*, 32
Ross, James 36
Rubha Reidh Lighthouse
  95
Rutherford, Roan 46

S

Sacrament House *16*
Sage, Revd Donald 35
Sandielands estate 32
Scatwell House 46
Scoraig 90
Scotsburn House 68
Scott, W Schomberg 93
Seaforth memorial *44*
Seaforth Sanatorium,
  Maryburgh 42
Shandwick (Old and New),
  Invergordon 7, 68
Shearer & Annand 47
Shieldaig 99
Smith, C H J 14
Smith, George 78
Smith, James 36, 58, 69,
  77, 78, 79, 82
Somerville, David 49, 56
South Erradale viaduct 98
Stevenson, Alan 23, 33-4
Stevenson, D A 95
Stevenson, Robert 74
Stewart, Lachlan 72
Stittenham 62

Strath, Gairloch 94
Strath Rory bridge 61
Strathcarron Railway Stn
  104
Strath Conon 46
Strathkanaird *87*
Strath More *88*, 89
Strathpeffer *3*, 7-50
  Ben Wyvis 49
  Nicholson Mackenzie
    Hospital 49
  Pavilion 49
  villas 48-9
Strome Castle 103
Stronach, Alexander 76
Struie 61

T

Tain 75-82
  Academy 78
  Bank of Scotland 79
  Collegiate Church 4
  Duthac House 78
  High Street 78-9
  Knockbreck Street 80
  Manse House 79
  Market 79
  Mercat Cross 77
  Morangie Road 80
  New Manse 79
  Quarry Lane 80
  Royal Hotel 77, 78
  Tolbooth 6, 76-7
  Town Hall 79
Tanera More 88
Tarbat 72
Tarbat House 67
Tarbat Ness Lighthouse
  74
Taylor, W 97
Telford, Thomas *4*, 5, 41,
  45, 46, 47, 61, 73, 86, 93,
  99
Thompson, Robert 77
Thoms & Nairn 64
Thoms, Andrew *70*
Tighnahinch 38
Torridon *6*, 98-9
  Coulin Lodge 98
  Loch Torridon Hotel 98
  Youth Hostel 99
Tucker, Thomas *26*
Tullich Farm, Lochcarron
  103
Tulloch Castle 56

U

Udrigle House 91
Ullapool 84-6
  Shore Street 85-6
Urquhart family 25
Urray 43-4

W

Wardrop & Reid 43
Watt, George 37
Weeks, H 102
Wester Ross 83-104
White, Edward 62
Williams, C R 33
Wyvis Lodge *63*

PICTORIAL GLOSSARY

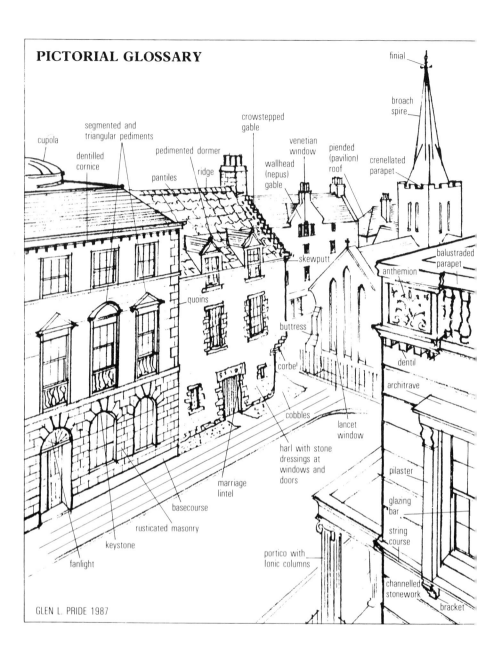

finial

broach spire

crowstepped gable

segmented and triangular pediments

cupola

dentilled cornice

pedimented dormer

venetian window

piended (pavilion) roof

crenellated parapet

wallhead (nepus) gable

pantiles

ridge

balustraded parapet

skewputt

anthemion

quoins

buttress

dentil

corbel

architrave

cobbles

lancet window

harl with stone dressings at windows and doors

pilaster

marriage lintel

glazing bar

basecourse

string course

rusticated masonry

portico with Ionic columns

keystone

channelled stonework

fanlight

bracket

GLEN L. PRIDE 1987

The RIAS Bookshops

Located in the centres of Edinburgh and Glasgow, the RIAS
Bookshops are the largest specialist architecture and building
bookshops in Scotland. There is a wide range of legal and technical
books in addition to volumes on design, including many beautiful
coffee table books. Both RIAS Bookshops now sell and accept Book
Tokens. Bookbank has been installed in our Edinburgh shop - we
are able to research and order all British books in print.

OTHER RIAS PUBLICATIONS

THE SCOTTISH THIRTIES *"McKean is never boring, far-fetched on
occasions, perhaps, but essentially on the side of the angels, balancing
visual acuity with perceptive, often witty comment. There are more than 400
black and white photographs, in addition to colour photographs and
drawings in this handsome volume"* THE SCOTSMAN

AUTHOR, CHARLES McKEAN. ISBN 0 7073 0494 6 **£8.50**

THE ARCHITECTURE OF THE SCOTTISH RENAISSANCE
*"... the European Renaissance had a profound and exciting impact on
Scottish culture - an impact that was expressed forcefully in the architecture
of the period"* THE SCOTSMAN

EDITOR, DR DEBORAH HOWARD. PAPERBACK **£2.00**

TAKE A LETTER *"...which I have thoroughly enjoyed and shall pass on to
my daughter, who is a youthful practising architect with much to learn
about real life"*

AUTHOR, SINCLAIR GAULDIE. PAPERBACK, ISBN 1873190 00 X. **£5.00**

WINNERS & LOSERS *"...should illustrate the fascinating, and
frequently controversial, course of architectural competitions in Scotland
since Craig's plan for the New Town of Edinburgh in 1766"*

AUTHOR, ROGER EMMERSON. PAPERBACK, ISBN 1 873190 03 4. **£2.95**

These RIAS books: and books on Scottish Architecture are all
available from the RIAS Bookshop,
15 Rutland Square, Edinburgh EH1 2BE
031-229 7545

and
545 Sauchiehall St, Glasgow G3 7PQ
041-221 6496

ARCHITECTURAL
— GUIDES —
TO SCOTLAND

The acclaimed RIAS/Landmark Trust series of
Architectural Guides to Scotland is essential reading for
people interested in the built history of the country.

SERIES EDITOR: CHARLES McKEAN

Already Published

EDINBURGH: by Charles McKean.

DUNDEE: by Charles McKean and David Walker.

STIRLING AND THE TROSSACHS: by Charles McKean 1985.

ABERDEEN: by W.A. Brogden 1986. Now in its 2nd editon.

THE SOUTH CLYDE ESTUARY: by Frank Arneil Walker 1986.

CLACKMANNAN AND THE OCHILS: by Adam Swan 1987.

THE DISTRICT OF MORAY: by Charles McKean 1987.

CENTRAL GLASGOW: by Charles McKean, David Walker,
Frank Arneil Walker 1989.

BANFF & BUCHAN: by Charles McKean 1990.

SHETLAND: by Mike Finnie 1990.

FIFE: by Glen Pride 1991.

ORKNEY: by Leslie Burgher 1991.

Forthcoming

NORTH CLYDE ESTUARY: THE MONKLANDS: CENTRAL
LOWLANDS: AYRSHIRE & ARRAN: BORDERS & BERWICK

The series is winner of the
Glenfiddich Living Scotland Award 1985.